Contents

Over the years, hundreds of artists have lent their talents to the pages of a Spider-Man comic. Each brings a new and different interpretation to the world famous wall-crawler.

FOREWORD

LIFE IS FUNNY! (As if you didn't know). I don't mean "Ha ha funny." I mean in the sense of odd, peculiar, strange.

You're probably wondering what this has to do with Spider-Man. Well, I'm glad you asked.

You see, before coming up with the idea for everyone's favorite web-swinger, I had already created The Fantastic Four and the incredible Hulk. And, after doing Spidey, Marvel and I then generously gifted an appreciative world with such characters as the X-Men, Daredevil, Iron Man, The Avengers, and... well, you get the idea.

So here's the point. Why is it that every new person I meet usually says something like, "Hey, aren't you the one who wrote Spider-Man?" I mean, they hardly ever ask me if I wrote the Hulk, or The Silver Surfer, or even Sgt. Fury and the Howling Commandos (for those of you with really long memories)? Nope, it's always, "Aren't you the one who wrote Spider-Man?"

Now, things like that make me think. Why is Spider-Man the first character that comes to mind when people mention Marvel or me? Over the years I've come up with a theory about that and now, because of my justly famed generosity, I'd like to share it with you.

I think Spidey has made such a lasting impression because he's possibly the most realistically human of all Super Heroes. He never has enough money, he's constantly beset by personal problems, and the world doesn't exactly applaud his deeds—in fact, most people tend to suspect and distrust him. In short, he's a lot like you and me.

There's another thing about Peter and his arachnid alter ego. When his series first started, way back in 1963, Peter was just a teenager, still in school. Most of the comic-book readers were teenagers as well, so that made it really easy for them to identify with him. You see, at that time all the comic-book Super Heroes were adults. The only teenagers in comics were the heroes' sidekicks. Well, I figured, "Where is it written that teenagers can only be sidekicks?" The answer, of course, was "Nowhere!" So, Spidey was probably the first comic-book hero that teenagers themselves could identify with.

Whoa, I think I omitted another important point. You may have noticed that Peter Parker never lived in Gotham City, or Metropolis, or any place that was obviously a fictional city. Nope, his very first story planted him firmly in Forest Hills, a part of New York City. So readers could really visualize him web-swinging around the streets of New York and its environs. It was just another element that gave Spidey a feeling of reality even though he was actually part of an imaginative comic-book universe.

Finally, there was the humor. I tried to make sure that our web-headed wonder was never without some sort of wisecrack or sharp retort, no matter how tense a situation might be. That, too, was an effort to be realistic because, as you know, most young people have a flip way of speaking. They're never as proper or pedantic as so many other heroes are portrayed. In fact, just between you and me, Spidey speaks a lot like I do. Or maybe I speak like he does. After a while, it's hard to tell who's imitating whom!

And there you have it. My take on the reason Spider-Man seems to have such an unshakable hold on the minds and emotions of so many readers. Even though I'm equally proud of the many other characters the mighty Marvel bullpen and I have been associated with over the years, I now feel I can understand why our wondrous wall-crawler is the first one people think of when they talk comics to me. And I hope I've succeeded in making it clearer to you, too.

If I haven't succeeded, that's okay. It makes me resemble poor ol' Peter Parker even more. None of us ever seems to get anything totally right!

But don't waste time worrying about us. There's a lot of story waiting for you on the pages ahead. So wiggle your webs and plunge right in. You know how your friendly neighborhood Spider-Man hates to be kept waiting!

Excelsior!

Stan Lee

One of the most iconic Super Heroes of all time, Spider-Man has leapt off the comic book page and into the mainstream. From big budget Hollywood films to action figures, from T-shirts to theme park attractions, from cartoons to a Broadway musical, Spider-Man's popularity is an indisputable fact, as is his status as Marvel's most notable creation.

INTRODUCING...

SPIDER-MAN

He swings through the air on merely a thin strand of webbing. He can climb up the side of a building as easily as he can walk down the street. Due to the irradiated bite of a spider, he has the proportionate strength of an arachnid, and can effortlessly lift nearly ten tons. He has an unexplainable precognitive sense of when danger is approaching. His reflexes, agility, and endurance pale the accomplishments of even the most dedicated athlete. He is the amazing Spider-Man.

But although Spider-Man possesses more power than most people could dream of, his alter ego, Peter Parker, is just a regular guy trying to make ends meet. Imbued with a strict moral code and a heightened sense of responsibility, Peter is always struggling to do the right thing, no matter the sacrifice involved. More than just the sum of his abilities, Spider-Man's strength and longevity come from the man beneath the mask, a man whose often-heard mantra dictates his every decision: "With great power there must also come—great responsibility!"

THE STORY OF SPIDER-MAN

"THIS SURE BEATS WAITING FOR A BUS!"

Stan Lee was toying with the idea of leaving comics. Fed up with the stagnant Super Hero format, Lee decided that before he quit, he'd take a whack at writing comics his way. From that simple idea sprang the Marvel Age of comics, and its main attraction—Spider-Man.

Stan Lee knew that he'd chanced upon something special when he concocted the idea of the Super Hero Spider-Man and his teenage alter ego Peter Parker. Before that time, almost every teenager in comics served as a sidekick. They were meant to be a younger voice that kids could relate to in order to better enjoy the adventures of the sidekick's mentor, the comic's star. Stan never liked sidekicks, but he saw potential in the concept of having a young lead character that a newer generation could claim as their own. So Lee placed Peter Parker squarely in high school, and to go even further, he decided to make Peter a bit of a bookworm. This in turn made the hero even more relatable. Peter Parker wasn't the type of high school student to try out for the football team, he was the kind who was more comfortable sitting on the sidelines reading a good book—or comic book, as the case may be.

Knowing he had a home run on his hands, Lee put a lot of consideration into deciding which artist to pair with. Although he usually partnered with the legendary Jack Kirby, after seeing Kirby's Spider-Man artwork, Lee decided Jack was making the character too heroic, and not the underdog Lee wanted to portray. While Jack sketched the cover, Lee turned to the brilliant Steve Ditko for the interiors, and everything fell smoothly into place. With the debut of *Amazing Fantasy* #15 in August 1962, the world met the amazing Spider-Man.

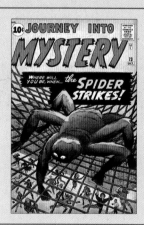

THE MAN-SPIDER?
Marvel had actually toyed with the idea of a Spider-Man before. In a story drawn by Jack Kirby called "Where Will You Be, When… the Spider Strikes!" and featured in *Journey Into Mystery* #73 (October 1961), an ordinary house spider is exposed to radiation and gains the abilities of a human. This monstrous spider even shot webbing, just like Spider-Man, but he was very different to the web-slinger we know and love.

STEVE DITKO

Gifted with an incredible design sense and an elegant and seemingly effortless storytelling technique, artist Steve Ditko added his distinct flair to Spider-Man, giving the comic a more down-to-Earth quality than many of its contemporaries. As if serving as the co-creator of Spider-Man wasn't enough for the artist, Ditko can also add the DC heroes Captain Atom, Question, Hawk, Dove, and Creeper to his impressive resume of creations, as well as another Marvel mainstay, the mystical Dr. Strange.

WHOP!

THE CREATORS

"AND NOW, YOU HIGH-VOLTAGE HEEL, I'LL GIVE YOU SOMETHING TO TALK ABOUT WHEN YOU WAKE UP BACK IN YOUR CELL! YOU CAN TELL THE OTHER CONS HOW IT FEELS TO BE ON THE RECEIVING END OF A KNOCKOUT PUNCH BY YOUR FRIENDLY NEIGHBORHOOD SPIDER-MAN!!"

SPIDER-MAN TO ELECTRO

STAN LEE

Stan "The Man" Lee might just be comics' biggest celebrity. Responsible for changing the face of Marvel, as well as the entire comic book industry in the 1960s, Lee has co-created hundreds of characters alongside landmark artists like Jack Kirby and Steve Ditko. The writer behind nearly all of Marvel's iconic heroes, from the Fantastic Four to Spider-Man to the Incredible Hulk to the X-Men, Lee worked at Marvel as a writer, editor, president, and chairman. Even when not acting as Marvel's guiding force, he has continued to serve as the company's inspiration.

August 1962

AMAZING FANTASY

12¢

15 AUG.

APPROVED BY THE COMICS CODE AUTHORITY

MC

INTRODUCING SPIDER MAN

THOUGH THE WORLD MAY MOCK PETER PARKER, THE TIMID TEEN-AGER...

...IT WILL SOON MARVEL AT THE AWESOME MIGHT OF SPIDER-MAN!

ALSO IN THIS ISSUE: AN IMPORTANT MESSAGE TO YOU FROM THE EDITOR—ABOUT THE NEW AMAZING!

AMAZING FANTASY #15

"Okay, world—better hang onto your hat! Here comes the Spider-Man!"

PETER PARKER

EDITOR-IN-CHIEF
Stan Lee

COVER ARTISTS
Jack Kirby and Steve Ditko

WRITER
Stan Lee

PENCILER
Steve Ditko

INKER
Steve Ditko

LETTERER
Art Simek

MAIN CHARACTERS: Spider-Man; Aunt May Parker; Uncle Ben Parker; The Burglar
MAIN SUPPORTING CHARACTERS: Sally; Flash Thompson; Crusher Hogan
MAIN LOCATIONS: Midtown High School; the Parker residence; Science exhibit, New York City; wrestling arena, New York City; TV studio, New York City; Acme warehouse, Queens, New York

BACKGROUND

Faced with the prospect of cancellation, the publisher of *Amazing Fantasy*, a comic packed with alien and monster stories, had nothing to lose when he agreed to let Stan Lee and Steve Ditko introduce a new and unconventional Super Hero to the world. In a mere eleven pages, writer-editor Stan Lee and artist Steve Ditko spun a tale that would take most current comic book writers around six issues to weave. It was to become the most famous story in Spider-Man's history: his origin.

Lee, together with Ditko, set the stage for Spider-Man's career by focusing on the true star, Peter Parker. Unlike many other comics of the day, which relied on super-heroics to lure in readers, Lee wanted his protagonist to be an everyman, an easily relatable high school student, who had to deal with the typical problems and troubles of adolescence outside of the hectic world of crime fighting.

And Lee and Ditko were right. Something in this tidy little piece of storytelling and artistry struck a chord with the readers, and although this was the last issue of *Amazing Fantasy*, the web-slinger proved so popular that less than a year later he was granted his own ongoing comic, *The Amazing Spider-Man*.

THE STORY

When bitten by a radioactive spider at a science exhibit, bookworm Peter Parker is transformed into the mysterious teen powerhouse sensation known as the amazing Spider-Man.

His classmates called him a "professional wallflower." The girls rejected him and the boys ridiculed and berated him every chance they got. But little did the students of Midtown High realize that soon enough they'd be calling Peter Parker "amazing."

But Peter's life wasn't all bad. Back in his modest Forest Hills home, Peter Parker had a support system in the form of his elderly Uncle Ben and Aunt May (**1**). Their kindness meant the world to him, and with their guidance, he often buried himself in his schoolwork, trying his best to ignore the cruel taunts of his high school peers (**2**).

On one such day, Peter was escaping his troubles at a science exhibit in New York City on radiology. Unbeknownst to the teen, a spider dangled into an active experiment, got doused by radioactive rays, and then bit Peter Parker on his hand (**3**). Feeling strange, Peter left the exhibit and wandered into the street, not noticing a car careering toward him. As if by instinct, the young man suddenly leapt out of the way, and managed to adhere to the side of a neighboring building (**4**).

After he accidentally crunched a steel pipe in his hand as if it were paper, Peter realized that the dying spider must have gifted him with an amazing new set of abilities (**5**). This was the opportunity he'd waited his entire life for. He quickly began to take advantage of his new powers, entering himself in an open-call wrestling match against a hulking brute called Crusher Hogan (**6**). Not wanting to reveal his identity to the general public, Peter donned a cheap mask as a disguise, and then easily defeated the wrestler in true showboat fashion. The match led to the cash prize, which led to Peter nabbing a publicity agent, which in turn led to the next big chapter in his life.

Peter crafted a bright costume and used his scientific knowledge to concoct wrist shooters and a revolutionary web-like adhesive (**7**). He dubbed himself Spider-Man and it wasn't long before he was starring in his own TV special. Happily strolling backstage after the first day's filming, Peter ignored the cries for help from a nearby policeman, and allowed a fleeing burglar to run right past him, unimpeded (**8**). It was a small incident, and Peter Parker assumed that it wasn't his problem.

Instead, Peter continued his career as Spider-Man, becoming a TV star and a national sensation. However, one night, when Peter was returning home from a personal appearance as Spider-Man, he was startled to find a police car parked in front of his house. The young man soon discovered his beloved Uncle Ben had been murdered (**9**), and that the culprit was held up at the Acme warehouse at the waterfront. In a fit of rage, Peter donned his Spider-Man costume, and swung across town to the dilapidated old building. The warehouse was surrounded by police, but they were powerless—the killer had plenty of places to hide and he would be able to pick them off one by one if they charged. Realizing it was only a matter of time before darkness fell, Spider-Man sprang into action. He quickly used his powers to capture and beat the criminal (**10**), only to discover that the man was the same burglar he had let escape from the TV studio just a few days earlier.

After webbing up the criminal for the police to find, Peter Parker walked slowly into the moonlight, overwhelmed with grief and guilt (**11**) and learning the most important lesson of his life: "With great power there must also come—great responsibility!"

> "If only I had stopped him when I **could** have! But I **didn't**—and now—Uncle Ben—is dead..."
>
> **PETER PARKER**

THE COSTUME

It was originally supposed to be just a simple stage costume. But when Spider-Man made the transition from show business to Super Hero, his famous red and blue attire soon became one of the most recognizable and celebrated costumes in the world. Peter Parker used his scientific expertise to create an ingenious costume with complex web-shooters and mask, and a belt packed with essential gadgets.

THE FIRST SPIDEY SUIT

When Peter Parker first designed his costume it wasn't for crime fighting. He essentially just needed an exciting look for his stage act. After learning that Midtown High's dance class was throwing out some old bodysuits, he slipped into the school after dark and found one that fit him. A few hours later, he had silk-screened a web pattern on the suit and made a skintight pair of gloves and boots. And Spider-Man was born.

As it turned out, Peter's knack for science was arguably rivaled by his design sense.

THE MASK

Born out of a need to hide his true identity, Spider-Man's mask might just be the most essential part of his uniform. The mask is thin and light, composed of a synthetic stretch fabric that matches the rest of his costume. While the lightweight material may come in handy on hot summer days, it can be prone to ripping, which is a problem that Peter always has to keep at the back of his mind while battling foes. A close encounter with the Lizard's claws or Kraven the Hunter's knife could expose his identity for the world to see, and put the lives of his loved ones in jeopardy.

Peter Parker created eyepieces using one-way mirrors he found in his school's drama class's prop box. These eyepieces hide Spider-Man's identity without hindering his vision.

While a full mask hides Peter's face from the world, it also plants a seed of distrust in the minds of the general public.

BELT UP

Beneath his costume's shirt, Spider-Man wears a belt that contains his spider-signal, spider-tracers, a miniature digital camera, and spare web cartridges. The major disadvantage of a skintight costume is that there's no room for Peter's street clothes. He either webs them into a ball attached to his back or he leaves them behind.

SPIDER-TRACER
One of Peter Parker's most useful inventions, a spider-tracer sends out a pulse that only Peter's spider-sense can detect.

WEB CARTRIDGES
Carrying extra web fluid is essential for Spider-Man, as his webbing can often mean the difference between life and death.

SPIDER-SIGNAL
Spidey often uses his spider-signal when patrolling at night. He projects his logo onto criminals to catch them off guard.

A MARVEL OF MODERN SCIENCE

Spider-Man's gloves and boots consist of a thin layer of material so that they do not inhibit his ability to stick to walls. Hidden under his gloves, with only the nozzles visible, are Spidey's web-shooters. These complex devices fire his revolutionary homemade web formula. Spider-Man is able to switch between different kinds of webbing with just a tap of his finger. The web-shooters can eject a single strand of webbing or a complex web (see pages 18–19).

With one of the most eye-catching costumes in all of Super Hero-dom, one would think Spider-Man wouldn't need to alter his uniform's iconic appearance. However, Peter Parker isn't above adopting a new suit if it will give him an advantage in a fight. From an insulated costume to protect himself from electricity, to a suit made of a living alien creature, Spider-Man's wardrobe has seen as many changes as the hero himself.

ARMORED COSTUME

Peter once donned a steel-plated version of his costume to battle a heavily armed team of villains known as the New Enforcers. The uniform was actually a pseudo-metallic composition that Peter created in the laboratories of Empire State University. But while the armor protected Spider-Man from heavy-caliber firearms, it greatly hindered his agility, and slowed him down. The suit was eventually destroyed by acid in battle.

STEALTH SUIT

Using the technology at Horizon Labs, Spider-Man developed a version of his costume that could be completely invisible by warping light and sound. The costume came equipped with lenses that allowed Spider-Man to see his own hands and feet, making movements much easier. The stealth suit was also completely impervious to sonic attacks.

BULLETPROOF COSTUME

After losing his spider-sense and getting shot with a bullet, Spider-Man used the facilities at Horizon Labs to create a bulletproof version of his costume. Flexible enough to not hinder Spider-Man's movement, the suit also employed magnetic webbing that fired out of the top of Spider-Man's wrists and blocked all radio frequencies.

FF UNIFORM

After Johnny Storm died, Spider-Man took his place as the fourth core member of the FF (the Future Foundation—the new incarnation of the Fantastic Four). Spidey was given a costume made of third generation unstable molecules, which could change design at will and had a black and white default setting. Although Spider-Man thought that the costume looked too much like the symbiote worn by his enemy Anti-Venom, being on the team meant so much to Spidey that he continued to wear the FF suit, keeping his complaints to a bare minimum.

WRESTLER COSTUME

Before Peter Parker had devised the costume and concept of Spider-Man, he first donned a mesh mask to hide his identity when he entered an open call wrestling match against hulking brute Crusher Hogan. Although the mesh mask worked as a disguise, it wouldn't cut it in the glamorous world of show business, and Peter went on to create his iconic blue and red costume.

COSMIC SPIDER-MAN

When a lab accident exposed Peter to an unknown energy source, his powers were upgraded and so was his costume. His new powers included flight, enhanced strength and senses, and the ability to shoot energy from his fingertips. In reality, the mysterious extra-dimensional entity known as the Enigma Force had bestowed upon Spider-Man its fabled Uni-Power, briefly turning Spidey into the latest in a long line of champions dubbed Captain Universe.

THE KNOCKOFF

On one occasion, when he was without his actual costume, Peter Parker was forced to take on the villain Overdrive while wearing a store-bought Halloween version of his famous uniform.

ALIEN COSTUME

Peter acquired his black costume while fighting on a far-off planet called Battleworld. This suit had a seemingly endless supply of webbing, and could change its appearance instantly. It seemed to respond to Peter's thoughts, and would slip over him whenever he wanted to go out web-swinging. But Peter eventually learned that the costume was an alien symbiote that wanted to form a permanent attachment to him. Even though he ultimately abandoned the alien suit, Spider-Man wore a cloth version for a time, given to him by the Black Cat.

AMAZING BAG-MAN

Stranded without clothes after discovering that his black costume was actually an alien symbiote, Peter found himself at the mercy of Human Torch. Unable to resist a joke at Spidey's expense, Johnny Storm let Spider-Man borrow a uniform that wasn't quite up to the wall-crawler's usual standards—although Johnny had a spare Fantastic Four costume, they were apparently short on masks.

SCARLET SPIDER

When Spider-Man's clone Ben Reilly returned to New York after years of travelling, he decided he couldn't escape his responsibility, and took up the identity of the Scarlet Spider. With a modified spider hoodie he'd purchased from a museum gift shop, and exterior web-shooters with a matching cartridge belt, Ben made his triumphant return to the Super Hero scene.

REILLY'S COSTUME

Peter Parker retired from costumed crime fighting for a brief time and turned over his duties to his clone Ben Reilly. Ben designed his own version of Peter's classic costume, with a much larger spider on his chest and a different design on his pants. As well as redesigning the web-shooters, he invented new weapons to add to his personal arsenal.

SIX-ARMED SPIDEY

At one point in his career, Peter's image drastically changed. In an attempt to live a normal life, Peter had developed a formula to remove his powers. Even though it hadn't been tested, he drank the liquid. When he came around, Peter felt a pain in his sides. He looked down as four extra arms burst through his costume! Peter turned to his friend Dr. Curt Connors, who helped him to develop a cure.

IRON SPIDER

In a campaign to win Peter Parker's favor, Tony Stark developed an "Iron Spider" costume made specifically for Peter's heroic needs. Able to deflect bullets, camouflage itself, and pick up radio frequencies, the suit gave Spider-Man key advantages in his war against crime, including a few extra arm-like appendages that extended out of the suit's back. While Peter eventually rejected the suit when he and Tony fell out over the Super Hero Civil War, the technology was later adapted by a group of government agents called the Scarlet Spiders.

Though Spider-Man tends to focus on his hands and feet when climbing up a wall, every part of his body has the same clinging ability.

He has the proportionate strength of a spider, the ability to adhere to nearly any surface, and an almost supernatural sense of when danger is approaching. But that's just the beginning of Spider-Man's amazing arachnid powers. His enhanced reflexes, speed, agility, and quick-healing abilities all combine to mean that Spider-Man ranks right up there with the most powerful of all the Super Heroes.

WITH GREAT POWER...

STRENGTH

Although not as strong as the Hulk, the mighty Thor, or even the Thing, your friendly neighborhood web-slinger should not be underestimated. He can bend a solid iron bar with his bare hands, lift almost 10 tons, and shatter a concrete wall with a single punch. And in a single, spider-powered spring, he can leap the height of three stories or the width of a highway.

SPEEDY SPIDEY

Even more impressive than his spiderlike strength is Spidey's amazing speed and agility. When it comes to quick-thinking, lightning-swift acrobatic stunts, the wall-crawling wonder is truly without equal. Spider-Man's reflexes operate up to 40 times faster than an average person. Even his healing abilities are greatly accelerated compared to non-powered individuals: he can recover in a day from a wound that would take a normal person weeks to recuperate from.

WALL-CRAWLING

No matter how smooth or slippery a surface may be, Spidey can attach himself to it. He just has to keep concentrating until he bonds with it. Unlike his spider-sense, the web-head's clinging power is strictly a conscious act. This comes in handy as nothing seems to unnerve a bad guy more than being approached by a certain webbed crime-fighter who is crawling up the side of a nearby wall.

SPIDER-SENSE

When faced with danger, Spider-Man is warned by a peculiar tingling sensation in the back of his skull. Over the years, Spidey has honed this sixth sense, forging it into one of the most useful tools in his arsenal. Able to detect anything from a fast-approaching bullet to tainted meat in a sandwich, Spidey's spider-sense can also be used as a radar to help him detect trouble in the city. Peter Parker has even developed special spider-tracers that are attuned to his spider-sense and can help him pinpoint foes, wherever they're hiding.

THE WEB HE WEAVES

Every spider needs a web, and Spider-Man is no exception. Although the radioactive spider that bit Peter Parker granted the young man many of the natural skills and strength of arachnids, it didn't give him the ability to produce webbing. Peter had to do that the old-fashioned way, with hard work and incredible ingenuity.

WEB FLUID

When Peter set out to create a web of his own, he used his high school's science laboratory after hours. Having studied multi-polymer compounds for a few years, he produced an adhesive fluid capable of imitating a spider's silk webbing. Extremely strong and durable, the web would dissolve after around one hour. While it would be no good as a practical adhesive to sell to chemical companies, the fluid was perfect for temporarily binding enemies of Spider-Man or swinging around the city.

WEB-SHOOTERS

While his web fluid was revolutionary and a marvel of modern chemistry, Peter didn't stop there. Without a way to fire his webs, Spider-Man was back to square one. As a solution to this problem, Peter designed two web-shooters that snap onto his wrists and can be fired by pressing his fingers to his palms. But not wanting to accidentally fire them every time he made a fist, Peter rigged the trigger so that he must tap twice in rapid succession, like a PC's mouse, to release his webbing.

The web-shooters that Peter has drafted each have nine rotating web fluid cartridges, along with the cartridge in use.

Underneath Spidey's costume is a belt that he designed to not only hold his camera and spider-signal, but also 30 extra cartridges of web fluid.

Spider-Man's web hardens upon exposure to air. Given sufficient thickness, one strand could bind the incredible Hulk and hold him prisoner, so Spidey rarely worries about it snapping under his own weight.

WEBMASTER

Always improving his technology, Spider-Man can now switch between different forms of webbing by the way he taps his trigger. With a short second tap he releases a thin cable-like strand that is perfect for web-swinging. A longer tap increases the strand's thickness for additional support, for example when binding a powerful foe like Norman Osborn. A series of brisk taps discharges many thin strands that form a fine spray, also good for blinding an opponent. If Spidey prolongs pressure on the trigger, web fluid squirts out in the form of an adhesive liquid.

ORGANIC WEBS

After a battle with the mysterious Queen, Spider-Man found himself transformed into a giant spider. While he was eventually able to change back into his old self, his brief metamorphosis was not without consequence. For some unknown reason, Spider-Man was then able to produce webbing from his own body. While it relieved some of the stress in Peter's daily life due to the fact that he no longer had to save up money to purchase the expensive chemicals needed for his webbing supply, the change was a bit off-putting for the wall-crawler, making him feel a little less human. This ability has faded away recently, however, and the details of the power loss remain a mystery.

After many hours of practice, Spidey has trained himself to use his webbing without conscious thought.

"SO, THEY LAUGHED AT ME FOR BEING A BOOKWORM, EH? WELL, ONLY A SCIENCE MAJOR COULD HAVE CREATED A DEVICE LIKE THIS!"

PETER PARKER

A WEB FOR ALL SEASONS

Over the years, Spider-Man has developed quite a few other uses for his webbing. He can easily use the webbing to form shapes like web-balls, bats, and bolos. Spider-Man has also been known to create more complex articles such as rafts, hang gliders, and skis. In addition, Spidey's normal webbing is also fairly heat-resistant and can easily withstand temperatures of 1,000°F (550°C). As a result, he's been known to wrap his fists in webbing as insulation to combat some of his more "hot-headed" foes. For extreme cases, he's even developed a webbing that resists temperatures of up to 10,000°F (5500°C).

PETER PARKER

The true face of Spider-Man, Peter Parker has seen more tragedy in his young life than most people three times his age. Racked with guilt and stress, Peter still often boasts a smile on his face, even though it's normally hidden by a skin-tight red mask.

PETER'S CHILDHOOD

Peter Parker was only a young boy when his parents, Richard and Mary Parker, died in a plane crash. He immediately moved in with his father's older brother and wife. Ben and May Parker were an elderly couple with no children of their own, and they raised Peter as if he were their son, but they rarely spoke about Peter's real parents. Peter became convinced that his parents had left him because of something he had done. Afraid of being abandoned, Peter worked hard to win his aunt and uncle's approval—though he didn't have to worry. Ben and May truly loved their nephew and would have done anything to please him.

As he grew older, Peter showed little interest in the hobbies of his peers. Although he would attend the occasional Mets game with his Uncle Ben, he never displayed any athletic prowess of his own. In fact, before he gained his spider-powers, Peter Parker had considerably less than average strength for a boy of his age. He had a fear of heights, too—even getting a book from the top shelf in the library resulted in his suffering severe symptoms of vertigo. He seemed ill-equipped for the often-harsh reality of teenage life.

When Peter's parents, Richard and Mary, were reported dead, Ben and May welcomed the orphaned child into their lives. The couple were living on a low income and had to make many sacrifices for the boy.

Peter's Uncle Ben enjoyed sharing his extensive comic collection with his nephew. Peter spent hours reading about courageous heroes and dreamed of being a costumed adventurer like Captain America, striking terror into the hearts of criminals.

MIDTOWN HIGH

In high school, Peter was an honor student, and his teachers thought very highly of him. The other students, however, had little time for a know-it-all like "Puny Parker." The girls thought he was quiet, and the boys considered him a wimp. Peter was painfully shy, and some of his fellow classmates misinterpreted his silence for snobbery. He had trouble making friends, but he never stopped trying. He often invited other students to join him at science exhibits or monster movies. But they usually responded with ridicule and almost never asked him to join them. But as he began his secret career as Spider-Man, Peter found a renewed sense of self-confidence, one his classmates slowly began to acknowledge.

> "I WISH I COULD BE A SUPER HERO. IT MUST FEEL SO GREAT TO BE ADMIRED BY THE POLICE AND THE PRESS..."
> PETER PARKER

COLLEGE STUDENT

Peter Parker graduated from Midtown High with the highest scholastic average in the school's history. He was thrilled to discover that he had won a full scholarship to Empire State University. Now secure in who he was, Peter immersed himself in his scientific studies despite web-swinging and a hectic social life. After graduating, Peter even took a job as a teaching assistant on campus to continue his postgraduate studies. Peter has never stopped learning and innovating, something that has served him incredibly well in his other life as the amazing Spider-Man.

Spider-Man ruined Peter's university graduation. In the week before the ceremony, Spidey was battling the Green Goblin and the Rocket Racer. He couldn't graduate with the rest of his class since he'd missed a required gym class.

THE MAN BEHIND THE MASK

Throughout his career as Spider-Man, Peter has always been torn between his sense of duty and the mixed feelings he has received from the public. This reception has varied from praise to outright condemnation. It has even driven him to the brink of despair, causing him to throw away his costume and renounce his alter ego. Nevertheless, his dedication to using his powers responsibly has always led to Peter donning his mask again in the hope that some day the world will learn to appreciate Spider-Man.

While Peter may have mastered the art of the quick change over the years, he finds it hard switching between his civilian and Super Hero identities, and often wishes he could just live a normal life.

FRIENDS & FAMILY

While Spider-Man has many trusted allies in his life as a hero, Peter Parker's world wouldn't be one worth fighting for without his family and circle of friends. In addition to former girlfriends turned lifelong companions, such as Betty Brant and Mary Jane Watson, Peter has had many people in his life who truly care about him. And even through difficult times, Peter has stood by those people closest to him.

UNCLE BEN PARKER

Born in Brooklyn, New York to a struggling working-class family, Ben Parker was a bright and happy boy who grew to never truly lose his inner child. He had a vivid imagination, collected comic books, and read science fiction—qualities and passions that he passed on to his nephew Peter, son of Ben's younger brother, Richard. After the tragic death of Peter's parents, Ben and his wife May took the young Peter in and raised him as their own. Loving and encouraging, Ben was Peter's best friend. It was Ben who instilled Peter with the knowledge that with great power, also comes great responsibility. And, ultimately, it was Ben's shocking death that inspired Spider-Man to become a hero.

RICHARD & MARY PARKER

Secretly operatives for the C.I.A., Peter's parents Richard and Mary Parker tried their best to give their only son as normal an upbringing as possible. But having been recruited by super spy Nick Fury, Richard had to have known that a normal life was going to be nearly impossible to accomplish. With adventures that involved fighting alongside heroes, including the man who would become known as Wolverine, Richard and Mary lived a dangerous life. And it was a life that was cut dramatically short when they died in a plane crash when Peter was just a young boy.

AUNT MAY JAMESON

May Parker didn't hesitate when she and her husband Ben were asked to take care of their nephew Peter for a few months while his parents were away on a business trip. And even more amazingly, she didn't balk at her new set of responsibilities when Peter's parents were killed and she and Ben became the boy's legal guardians. Instead she saw taking care of Peter as an opportunity to achieve her lifelong dream of becoming a parent.

But with so much death in her life, May couldn't help but be overprotective of Peter Parker. While she showered him with love every chance she had, she also worried constantly about his health and wellbeing, an almost obsessive behavior that grew even worse after Ben was murdered. These days, May has finally learned to relax, a quality she's picked up from her new husband, J. Jonah Jameson Sr.

RANDY ROBERTSON

Peter Parker met Randy Robertson during his days as a college student at Empire State University. Introduced by Randy's father and Peter's employer Joe Robertson of the *Daily Bugle*, Randy and Peter hit it off and began a friendship that continues to this day. Originally a political activist and avid protestor, Randy's personality has mellowed over the years, and he has gone from a career in social work to that of an actor. Lately, Randy has been dating one of Peter's friends at the *Daily Bugle*, Norah Winters.

FLASH THOMPSON

Peter Parker didn't have many friends in high school, and one of the main reasons for that, was the work of his greatest adversary, Eugene "Flash" Thompson. An all-round athlete, gifted with good looks and popularity, high school bully Flash enjoyed making Peter's life miserable, ironically even as he was a staunch supporter of Spider-Man. While Peter and Flash clashed repeatedly, their animosity would blossom into friendship when they later found themselves attending the same college. While not above giving Peter a hard time on occasion, Flash is very aware of how loyal a friend Peter has become, sticking by him even through his troubles with alcohol and the terrible wartime injury that cost Flash his ability to walk.

VIN GONZALES

Vin Gonzales, a tough New York City cop, was Peter Parker's roommate. But he is not a fan of Spider-Man. While Peter's and Vin's friendship was a bit rocky from the start due to Peter's secret escapades as Spider-Man, it got worse when Vin was discovered as part of a conspiracy to frame the wall-crawler. Vin was sentenced to jail time and Peter began dating the object of Vin's affection, Carlie Cooper. But despite their differences, Vin shares Peter's sense of responsibility, and willingly paid the price for his actions.

HARRY OSBORN

When Harry Osborn first met Peter Parker at college, Peter snubbed him completely. Always lost in his own world of worry, at the time Peter was more concerned about the health of his sickly aunt than meeting classmates at his new college. But Harry gave him the benefit of the doubt and a second chance, and the two became fast friends. They later even became roommates when Harry's father, the wealthy mogul Norman Osborn, paid for the boys' luxury apartment. Peter has seen Harry through several serious problems, including a lingering drug addiction, as well as a life as the heir to the Super Villain legacy of the Green Goblin. While many people would have given up hope in their friend years ago, Peter has always done just the opposite, convinced that Harry Osborn is truly worth saving.

J. JONAH JAMESON SR.

Peter first met J. Jonah Jameson Sr. as Spider-Man when the villainous Shocker trapped the two in a subway train alongside several other innocent bystanders. Peter was impressed by the man then, and continued to be impressed with him as he stayed in Peter's life and eventually married his aunt. Always approving of Jay and May's relationship, Peter has a hard time understanding how such an honorable man like Jay Jameson could sire a child as scheming and self-centered as J. Jonah Jameson Jr., publisher of the *Daily Bugle* and Spider-Man's worst critic.

THE
DAILY BUGLE

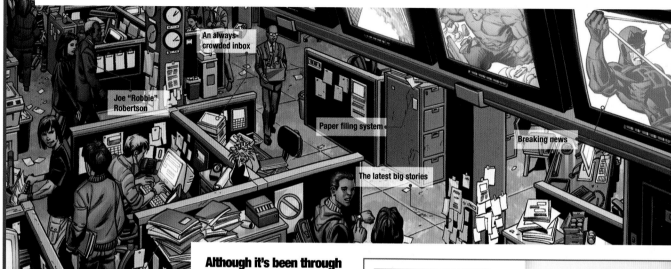

An always-crowded inbox

Joe "Robbie" Robertson

Paper filing system

Breaking news

The latest big stories

Research files

Although it's been through about as many changes as Spider-Man himself, the *Daily Bugle* is one of the world's most trusted tabloid newspapers. The newspaper has been a New York City institution since 1897, and is manned by an ever-changing staff that has included publisher J. Jonah Jameson and photographer Peter Parker.

Spider-Man takes photographs by webbing up an automatic camera in strategic locations before his fights.

A NEW YORK ICON

In letters 30 feet high, the original *Daily Bugle* office proudly displayed its name with a lack of subtlety that could only be matched by the passion of its editorial page and the flamboyance of its publisher, J. Jonah Jameson. The paper itself is a picture-dominated tabloid that goes for the jugular. Its photos are often graphic and shocking, and its stories are powerful.

Recently, when Jameson suffered a near-fatal heart attack, his wife sold the *Daily Bugle* to publisher Dexter Bennett, who renamed the paper *The DB*. Many of the staff left to work at a new start-up venture, *Front Line*. While Bennett's *The DB* focused on exploitative, paparazzi-styled articles, *Front Line* continued to retain the integrity that the *Daily Bugle* had always been known for.

PETER PARKER: ACE PHOTOGRAPHER

J. Jonah Jameson didn't hesitate to buy photos from the teenage Peter Parker, especially since Parker seemed to have a special talent for catching Spider-Man in action. Peter's first pictures appeared in Jameson's early venture, *Now Magazine*, but Jonah soon began to feature his work in the *Daily Bugle*, helping jumpstart the teen's career. Despite Peter's consistent success in getting photos of Spider-Man, Jonah has never discovered the young man's secret.

THE STAFF

J.J. JAMESON

He may appear to be a grouchy, self-centered old skinflint on the outside, but peel away his protective layers and you will discover that the real J. Jonah Jameson is actually even worse. The *Daily Bugle* publisher and staunch anti-Spider-Man activist never tires of hearing his own voice, and he'll gladly give you the opinions he thinks you ought to have. Although he no longer works at the *Daily Bugle*, Jameson will undoubtedly be back in the paper business before too long.

Jameson left the newspaper business behind when he became New York City's mayor.

JOE ROBERTSON
Usually the voice of compassion and reason, Joe Robertson worked as Jameson's right-hand man and conscience, before graduating to become the paper's Editor-in-Chief.

BETTY BRANT
Peter Parker's first real girlfriend and former *Bugle* secretary, Betty is a talented reporter whose dedication to her job has sometimes cost her her friends.

NORAH WINTERS
Full of energy and determination, Norah Winters is quickly becoming one of the *Bugle*'s top reporters, and has often partnered Peter Parker.

FREDERICK FOSWELL
Although a trusted *Daily Bugle* employee, Frederick Foswell led a double life as the criminal mastermind and ringleader known as the Big Man.

THOMAS FIREHEART
Secretly the vigilante the Puma, Thomas Fireheart once purchased the *Bugle* and wrote pro-Spider-Man articles as a way of paying a perceived debt to the wall-crawler.

BEN URICH
The *Bugle*'s star reporter and the founder of rival paper, *Front Line*, Urich is an ally of both Spider-Man and Daredevil, and known for his daring stance against corruption.

NED LEEDS
One-time husband of Betty Brant, Ned Leeds served as a reporter for the *Daily Bugle* before being brainwashed into becoming Hobgoblin by the original Hobgoblin.

DEXTER BENNETT
Purchasing the *Daily Bugle* and renaming it *The DB*, Dexter Bennett seemingly had none of the integrity of his predecessor, J. Jonah Jameson.

GLORY GRANT
Formerly a secretary to J.J. Jameson and Joe Robertson at the *Daily Bugle*, Glory Grant has moved up in the world, and is now an assistant to Mayor Jameson.

LANCE BANNON
A photographic rival of Peter Parker's, Lance Bannon had a healthy career under J.J. Jameson due to his unflattering photos of Spider-Man.

PHIL URICH
Nephew of Ben Urich, Phil has been dabbling in some web reporting for the newest incarnation of the *Bugle*, while moonlighting as the villain Hobgoblin.

JACOB CONOVER
Another in the long list of corrupt *Daily Bugle* employees, reporter Jacob Conover was known in criminal circles as a ringleader named the Rose.

THE DB BUILDING

Under Dexter Bennett's watch, *The DB* building was attacked and razed by the Super Villain known as Electro. Losing all interest in the business and the expense it would take to get the paper back on its feet, Bennett sold the company back to J. Jonah Jameson. In a moment of almost uncharacteristic generosity, Jameson then gifted the name of the *Daily Bugle* to *Front Line*, instantly giving the underground paper the name recognition it needed.

Although Peter Parker is best known as a photographer, snapping pictures for the *Daily Bugle* was not really his dream profession. With a genius-level scientific intellect and a desire to pass that knowledge onto others, photography was not so much a life goal for Peter, but rather a way for him to earn money to care for his sickly Aunt May and to pay his many bills.

MR. PARKER

It seems that Peter Parker had always held the idea of being a teacher in the back of his mind. So when the opportunity arose to teach science at his old school, Midtown High, Mr. Parker decided it was the perfect opportunity to make an impact on the lives of other promising students, just as his teachers had made such a difference in his life. Although his teaching career ended sooner than he'd have liked due to the attention he received at the time of the Super Hero Civil War, Spider-Man occasionally subs at the Avengers Academy when he finds himself missing the blackboard.

THE RIGHT-HAND MAN

As a huge fan of science and its innovators, Peter had long been in awe of his fellow Super Hero and Avenger Tony Stark, also known as the Golden Avenger Iron Man. In the days preceding the controversial Super Hero Civil War, Peter served as Tony's aide of sorts, learning directly from Stark's genius as he accompanied him on trips and lived in Tony's plush Stark Tower.

Peter was shocked to learn that J.J. Jameson was able to release *Webs* without his permission, paying him a paltry $100 "gratitude fee."

THE RELUCTANT AUTHOR

Peter's career as a photojournalist peaked when a collection of his Spider-Man photographs was released in a hardbound book entitled *Webs: Spider-Man in Action*. While the book was just another money-making stunt by the *Daily Bugle* publisher J. Jonah Jameson, and didn't land Peter any real money, it did give him the opportunity to get paid for a book-signing tour and to enjoy his very own 15 minutes of fame.

Spider-Man made a surprise appearance on the book tour after chasing the jewel thief, Black Fox.

THE OVERACHIEVER

When Peter decided to continue his education, he became a teaching assistant at Empire State University. Although he often found himself extremely overworked due to juggling life as Spider-Man and also as a photographer, Peter met a lot of good friends through his co-workers and found his work with the undergrads particularly rewarding.

GLOBE TROTTER

After years of being treated like he was on the lowest rung of the ladder by J.J. Jameson at the *Daily Bugle*, Peter found the respect he deserved for a time as Chief Photographer at the *Daily Globe*. The *Bugle*'s biggest rival, the *Globe* is more balanced in its reporting of Spider-Man.

HORIZON LABS

All through his life, Peter Parker was never able to live up to his full potential when not in costume as Spider-Man. But with the help of J. Jonah Jameson's wife Marla, Peter was given the opportunity to shine when she introduced him to Max Modell, the head of Horizon Labs, a research facility that creates revolutionary technology. After impressing Modell, Peter was offered a job at Horizon's coveted think tank.

Peter proved his merit on a tour of Horizon Labs and landed a job in the inner think tank.

BEYOND THE HORIZON

Peter's current employer, Horizon Labs, is a state of the art research facility. Laid out in a way to inspire its designers and engineers, the workspace has a social atrium area where its staff can mingle and swap ideas. It also houses the labs of its inner think tank where Horizon's star staffers can indulge in their most bizarre experiments to help the company—and technology— advance. As a member of this inner circle, Peter is free to design new technology for Spider-Man, as well as for the world.

MAX MODELL
The man behind Horizon Labs, Max Modell believes Peter is designing Spider-Man's technology, but doesn't know that he is actually the wall-crawler.

GRADY SCRAPS
A fellow think tank member, Grady Scraps doesn't seem like the most serious student of the sciences, although his incredible work proves otherwise.

BELLA FISHBACH
With an environmentally friendly mind and an eye towards our planet's future, Bella Fishbach is Horizon's resident green specialist, working in the inner think tank.

SAJANI JAFFREY
Another member of Horizon Labs' inner think tank, Sajani Jaffrey is the resident xenologist, specializing in alien biology, chemistry, and technology.

UATU JACKSON
All-around wonderkid Uatu Jackson graduated from high school at the age of ten before becoming the youngest member of Horizon Labs' think tank.

"THE MORE I RISK MY LIFE... THE MORE DEADLY CHANCES I TAKE... THE LESS GOOD IT SEEMS TO DO! WITH ALL MY STRENGTH... WITH ALL MY POWERS... WHY CAN'T I EVER MAKE THINGS RIGHT?"

PETER PARKER

PARKER'S PROBLEMS

Compared to fighting Super Villains and narrowly avoiding death as Spider-Man, you would think that life as Peter Parker would be a breeze. But, truth be told, Peter's daily struggles are every bit as challenging as those of his alter ego. It seems Peter is truly cursed with the infamous "Parker Luck."

GUILT

Since the death of his parents, Peter Parker has been plagued with guilt. Despite having nothing to do with the death of Richard and Mary Parker, young Peter instinctively thought their absence was a result of his behavior. As time passed and Peter lost more of the people in his life, including his beloved Uncle Ben, to tragedies he believed he could have or should have prevented, those issues only intensified.

GIRLS

Things never seem to be going smoothly in the romance department for Peter Parker. From his early experiences of being shunned by the objects of his affection in high school, to his near marriage to Mary Jane Watson, Peter has had his share of dating troubles. As long as he continues being Spider-Man and having to make up excuses to hide his secret identity, he can only expect more problems in the future.

AUNT MAY

Having lost his parents and his Uncle Ben at such an early age, Peter has come to realize how much his Aunt May means to him. And unfortunately, May has been plagued with health problems for a good portion of Peter's life. With hospital bills often piled up alongside other accumulated debt, Peter was constantly worried about May's wellbeing, and was forced to take several jobs to help her as best he could.

SPIDER-MAN

Strangely enough, Peter's biggest problem is probably Spider-Man himself. All Peter ever really wanted was to lead a normal life and be happy. Although he has managed to carve out a lot of happiness amidst the tragedy in his world, Peter has led anything but a normal existence. Compelled to be Spider-Man for the sake of the greater

good, Peter is constantly skipping out on friends or loved ones to battle the latest Super Villain or save a family from a towering inferno. Although he loves web-swinging and helping others, Peter knows that his double life is a giant roadblock in his personal life.

When a SPIDER-MAN *Loves* a *Woman*

To hear Peter Parker tell it, he's never had a lucky day in his life. But for someone who sees himself to be the victim of constant bad fortune, both Peter and his alias Spider-Man have certainly had more than their fair share of romantic encounters. With so many women vying for Peter's attention, it's hard not to see Spider-Man as one of the luckiest Super Heroes in the universe.

DEBRA WHITMAN
Debra Whitman desperately wanted her relationship with her fellow graduate student Peter Parker to develop into something more than friendship, but Peter never realized how much she truly liked him. Although they went on several dates, their romance never reached the committed level that Debra was hoping for, partly due to Peter's hectic secret life as Spider-Man.

Betty Brant
Peter's first steady girlfriend Betty Brant entered his life when he was viewed as just a shy bookworm by his fellow high school classmates. Forced to drop out of high school and become a secretary at the *Daily Bugle* to support her family, Betty understood and empathized with Peter's worries. They fell in love, but Peter's dual identity took its toll on their relationship. Unhappy with the risks Peter seemed to be taking for his job as a photographer, Betty began dating reporter Ned Leeds.

MARCY KANE
Back when Peter Parker was a teaching assistant at Empire State University, he met and briefly dated Marcy Kane, a graduate student. What Peter wasn't aware of at the time was that Marcy was actually an alien from the planet Contraxia. She had been sent to Earth to try to find a method to save her star system.

LIZ ALLAN
Liz Allan was one of the most popular and attractive girls at Peter's school, Midtown High. She developed a crush on Peter as the shy and bookish teen slowly grew out of his shell. However, their flirtation fizzled into friendship territory, and she later went on to date and marry Peter's friend Harry Osborn, with whom she had a son, Normie.

Although Peter's relationship with Betty Brant ended, the two remained dedicated friends.

The one-time fiancée of Peter Parker, Mary Jane Watson will forever be "the one that got away."

Mary Jane Watson
Peter Parker certainly hit the jackpot when it came to Mary Jane Watson. The beautiful niece of Peter's neighbor and Aunt May's best friend Anna Watson, Mary Jane discovered Peter's dual identity even before they went on their first date. Hiding under the façade of a fun-loving party girl, MJ was more complicated than she'd ever let on, a fact adult Peter only discovered when they finally began their years-long romance.

SARAH RUSHMAN
Sarah Rushman, a waitress and student at Empire State University, met Peter at a party, and the two decided to go out on a date. However, their affair quickly ended when Peter discovered that Rushman was actually the violent mutant known as Marrow. She had been brainwashed into her civilian identity of Sarah Rushman by the government intelligence agency S.H.I.E.L.D.

Gwen Stacy

For a time, Gwen Stacy was the love of Peter Parker's life. Peter and Gwen began a college romance that was cut much too short when the Green Goblin hurled the innocent girl off the top of the Brooklyn Bridge. Gwen's death has affected Peter profoundly, and he has tortured himself on many a sleepless night, replaying the horror in his head. He still finds himself daydreaming about their life together and what could have been.

Peter was convinced he would spend the rest of his life with his dream girl, Gwen.

Spidey's on-off love interest Black Cat shares his sense of adventure.

Black Cat

A cat burglar by heritage, Felicia Hardy always lived a dangerous life, and her relationship with Spider-Man wasn't that different. She felt a kinship with the lone hero, but quickly became obsessed with him. Not only did she wear the black cat costume to attract Spider-Man's attention, but she also kept a shrine to his honor, and even reformed her criminal ways to stay close to the hero. The two have had an on-off relationship for years, with neither truly getting what they need out of it. Felicia had difficulty understanding Spider-Man's need to live a civilian life.

While she loves the "spider," the Black Cat isn't really that keen on the "man."

LILY HOLLISTER

Peter first met fun-loving socialite Lily Hollister through her boyfriend, Harry Osborn. Living a double life as the villain Menace, Lily once kissed Peter in order to hide her secret identity, but it was a gesture that caused Parker more grief—he felt terrible for kissing his good friend's girlfriend.

MICHELE GONZALES

The sister of his former roommate Vin Gonzales, Peter Parker was caught off guard when Michele Gonzales moved in with him and became his roommate. The two had a few brief affairs before realizing that they weren't a good fit for each other.

MS. MARVEL

Spider-Man's fellow Avenger Ms. Marvel was initially annoyed by team-ups with the wall-crawler. But the two became friends when Spider-Man helped her on missions, and as they've grown closer, Ms. Marvel has developed feelings for her teammate that either has yet to fully explore.

Carlie Cooper

Peter's most recent love interest Carlie Cooper is a forensic officer for the New York Police Department and Lily Hollister's friend. While it took Peter some time to fully notice and appreciate Carlie, once they finally connected, the couple realized how much they had in common, including a mutual love for science.

AMAZING FRIENDS

New York City is a crowded town, and no one knows that better than Spider-Man. In a city that is home to millions of people, it's no surprise that the web-spinner has met dozens of other heroes over the years. Through the course of his career, Spidey has teamed up with other Super Heroes, and he has even made a few friends from those he once considered enemies.

SILVER SABLE

Silver Sable is one of the toughest mercenaries that Spider-Man has ever come across. Having adopted her father's profession as a bounty hunter and taken it to the next level of profitability and efficiency, Silver and her team of employees—the Wild Pack—will use their expertise in combat, gymnastics, and martial arts to take down any criminal for a hefty price. Silver is usually, but not always, an ally of Spider-Man.

MORBIUS

When Dr. Michael Morbius discovered that he was dying from a rare blood disease, he attempted to treat his illness with electroshock therapy and substances found in the bodies of vampire bats. The radical treatment transformed Morbius into a living vampire of sorts with enhanced strength and bloodlust. After clashing with Spider-Man several times, the two eventually became allies.

VENOM

Peter Parker's former school bully, Eugene "Flash" Thompson has always looked up to Spider-Man. The founder of a Spider-Man fan club, Flash has never wavered in his support of the world-famous wall-crawler. So when he lost his legs while serving his country, Flash didn't hesitate when the government offered him not only a chance to regain his mobility, but also to possess superpowers, by donning a living alien symbiote suit as the new Venom.

MADAME WEB

When Julia Carpenter was injected with a mysterious serum that gave her spider powers, she became known as Spider-Woman. A longtime crime fighter and ally of Spider-Man, Julia was also a member of several Super Hero teams, including the Avengers, Force Works, and Omega Flight. Having adopted many different monikers, including Arachne, she recently became known as Madame Web, after developing extra precognitive abilities.

SCARLET SPIDER

The notorious clone of Peter Parker, Ben Reilly adopted a crime-fighting identity of his own when he realized that he could not escape the responsibility that came with possessing all of the same powers and memories as the real Peter Parker. Dubbed the Scarlet Spider by the press, Ben fought valiantly alongside his "brother" and even in place of him when Spider-Man retired briefly. But Ben nobly sacrificed his own life to his cause.

PUMA

A master of martial arts with enhanced animalistic abilities, Thomas Firehart now uses his skills and powers as a contract mercenary, after conquering the world of corporate business. With his own strict moral code and a need to repay his own debts, the Puma has fought alongside Spider-Man at times. Although they often met as enemies in the past, the Puma has gained great respect for the wall-crawler.

SPIDER-WOMAN

The original Spider-Woman, Jessica Drew, has appeared on and off in Spider-Man's life, although she and the wall-crawler have spent the majority of their careers pursuing very different paths. An agent of the government peacekeeping force S.H.I.E.L.D., and later a double agent for the terrorists Hydra, Drew also joined the Avengers where she and Spider-Man are now regular partners.

TOXIN

When the serial-killing alien symbiote called Carnage gave birth to a spawn, the offspring took roost in the body of Patrick Mulligan, a New York City police officer. Although Mulligan is aware of his symbiote's corrupting influence, he has managed to keep control of the creature, and has even created an identity for himself as the crime-fighting Toxin—the first symbiote that Spider-Man considers an ally.

JACKPOT

When Jackpot first appeared, Spider-Man thought it might be Mary Jane Watson lurking under the costume. However, he soon deduced that she was Alana Jobson, a regular civilian who used Mutant Growth Hormone to give herself enhanced abilities. When Alana died, Sara Ehret adopted the Super Hero role, reluctantly realizing that her own superhuman powers were a gift she could not squander. Like Alana before her, she became an ally of Spider-Man.

ANTI-VENOM

Eddie Brock's brutal vigilante career as the villainous Venom landed him the reputation as one of Spider-Man's greatest foes. But after losing his alien symbiote suit and encountering the Super Villain Mister Negative, Eddie mysteriously manifested the rapid healing powers of Anti-Venom. Calling a truce with Spider-Man, he teamed up with the wall-crawler to battle mutual foes.

BLACK CAT

Influenced by the career of her cat burglar father, Felicia Hardy adopted the identity of the thieving Black Cat. After her adventures led her into a few conflicts with the wall-crawler, Felicia eventually changed her ways, using her "bad luck" powers to aid Spider-Man, and even becoming his girlfriend. While they're no longer romantically entangled, Spider-Man and the Black Cat still partner occasionally, something Spidey struggles to keep strictly professional.

SPIDER-GIRL

While she was reluctant to adopt the Super Hero name Spider-Girl, Anya Corazon wasn't so hesitant when it came to putting on a costume and fighting crime. The benefactor of powers from a mystical spider cult, Anya began her career as the hero Araña soon after she gained her abilities. But it wasn't until after Kraven's Grim Hunt of spider heroes, where she had fought alongside Spider-Man, that she fully accepted the role and costume of Spider-Girl.

PROWLER

Embarking on a criminal career to prove himself after he lost his job as a window washer, Hobie Brown donned the costume of the Prowler and soon crossed paths with Spider-Man. Later reforming his illegal ways, Hobie teamed up with Silver Sable as well as several other reformed villains. He and Spider-Man have partnered on several occasions, and the Prowler even designed some new technology for one of the wall-crawler's missions.

THE FF

When the Human Torch, one of the founding members of the super-powered Fantastic Four, died, it seemed the Fantastic Four would be no more. However, one of the Human Torch's final requests was for Peter Parker to take his place on the team. Spider-Man accepted the role, only to learn that the team's patriarch, Mr. Fantastic, had decided to rebrand the team. Now called the FF (the Future Foundation), the team has become much more than a group of four crime fighters. It is a collective of young people dedicated to making the world a better place.

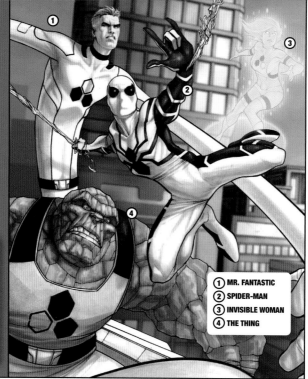

KEY DATA

TEAM'S FIRST APPEARANCE:
The Fantastic Four #579
(July 2010)

FOUNDER: Mr. Fantastic

ISSUE SPIDER-MAN JOINED:
FF #1 (May 2011)

BASE: The Baxter Building,
New York City, New York

1. MR. FANTASTIC
2. SPIDER-MAN
3. INVISIBLE WOMAN
4. THE THING

TEAM PLAYER

Although a loner for the majority of his career, Spider-Man has recently become a major believer in the power of teamwork. He currently serves as a member of three Super Hero groups at the same time: the FF, Avengers, and New Avengers.

THE NEW FANTASTIC FOUR

Early in Spider-Man's career, the wall-crawler helped to found a new, but short-lived incarnation of the Fantastic Four. The original members of the Fantastic Four had been taken captive by an alien shape-shifting Skrull named De'Lila, who then manipulated Spider-Man, Wolverine, the Hulk, and Ghost Rider into forming a new Super Hero team.

KEY DATA

TEAM'S FIRST APPEARANCE:
The Fantastic Four #347
(December 1990)

FOUNDING MEMBERS:
Spider-Man, Hulk, Ghost Rider,
Wolverine

ISSUE SPIDER-MAN JOINED:
The Fantastic Four #347

BASE: Mobile

1. GHOST RIDER
2. HULK
3. SPIDER-MAN
4. WOLVERINE

THOR

SPIDER-MAN

HAWKEYE

KEY DATA

TEAM'S FIRST APPEARANCE:
The Avengers #1 (September 1963)

FOUNDING MEMBERS: Thor, Iron Man, Hulk, Ant-Man, the Wasp

ISSUE SPIDER-MAN JOINED:
The Avengers (4th series) #1 (July 2010)

BASE: Avengers Tower, New York City, New York

IRON MAN

SPIDER-WOMAN

WOLVERINE

CAPTAIN AMERICA

AVENGERS

They're the world's greatest heroes. The mightiest assembly of super beings that the planet has ever known. They're the Avengers, and finding a place on their roster is the crowning achievement in any hero's career. Although Spider-Man was made a reserve Avenger years ago, he didn't achieve full membership to the ever-changing team until much later. These days, the web-crawler serves on two branches of the team, both with the icons of the Avengers as well as the heroes in the New Avengers.

1. THE THING
2. LUKE CAGE
3. MS. MARVEL
4. WOLVERINE
5. SPIDER-MAN

NEW AVENGERS

The New Avengers originally banded together after a prison breakout at the Vault, a New York maximum security penitentiary, and they were the first incarnation of the Avengers that Spider-Man joined on a full-time basis. The group faced clandestine organizations, alien threats, and mutant manifestations. But no threat tore at the team like the Super Hero Civil War, which split the New Avengers into two factions—the government-supported Mighty Avengers and the underground Secret Avengers. Spider-Man took his place with the underground faction, and has remained with the team since its rebirth under the leadership of Luke Cage.

KEY DATA

TEAM'S FIRST APPEARANCE:
New Avengers #1 (January 2005)

FOUNDING MEMBERS: Captain America, Iron Man, Luke Cage, Spider-Woman, Spider-Man

ISSUE SPIDER-MAN JOINED:
New Avengers #3 (March 2005)

BASE: Avengers Mansion, New York City, New York

SPIDEY TEAM-UPS

While it took Spider-Man years before he was recruited to an actual Super Hero team, he was partnering with other heroes almost right from the beginning of his career. From the gruff Wolverine to the welcoming Firestar, Spidey found a way to earn each hero's trust and respect.

Spider-Man had grown up reading about Captain America, so partnering with the living legend was a bit surreal.

CAPTAIN AMERICA

An icon in the world of Super Heroes, Spider-Man was more than a little intimidated by Captain America when they first teamed up. Even though Spider-Man's reputation was spotty with the police and the press, Captain America gave the fledgling hero the benefit of the doubt when they battled the Rogue Scholars, a group of time-traveling scientists, and a mutual respect was born.

WOLVERINE

On paper, they seem like an unlikely pairing. One's a natural rebel who's bucked the system for over a century—a wandering mutant with a fight-first mentality. The other's a wise-cracking bookish type whose guilt complex causes him to do the right thing above even his own personal safety. But despite their differences, Wolverine and Spider-Man have found themselves partners on many occasions. From fighting through jungles off the coast of Japan, to local Manhattan bar brawls, these two make an excellent team, something even Wolverine would admit—when Spider-Man isn't around, of course.

FIRESTAR & ICEMAN

Firestar, a former member of the Super Hero team dubbed the New Warriors, has partnered with Spidey on several occasions, most notably when she helped to curb the bloody massacre that was orchestrated by the Super Villain Carnage. Spidey and Iceman have also crossed paths a few times, both with and without Iceman's X-Men teammates. But the three found that they worked best as a trio, conquering threats like Videoman. Their teaming even led to a romance between Iceman and Firestar, but it was rather short-lived due to the two mutants' conflicting personalities.

HUMAN TORCH

Spider-Man and Johnny Storm didn't really like each other at first. Spidey always thought that the Fantastic Four's young hotshot, the Human Torch, was too arrogant. But over the years, with dozens of team-ups under their belts, the two discovered that they were actually more like brothers. So much so, that when the Human Torch died, his last wish was for Spider-Man to take his place on the Fantastic Four.

DAREDEVIL

Blind lawyer Matt Murdock, also known as Daredevil, first teamed up with Spider-Man when they took on the villainous Ringmaster and his Circus of Crime. With foes like the notorious Kingpin in common, the two crime fighters often found themselves joined in battle, and grew to become true friends. On one occasion, the pair even ended the partnership of two of their greatest respective villains: the Vulture and the Owl.

CLOAK & DAGGER

When two teen runaways were kidnapped and experimented upon with a powerful drug, they manifested bizarre powers. Now young Super Heroes, Cloak absorbs criminals into the darkness that engulfs him, while Dagger strikes them down with daggers of light. The pair met Spider-Man early in their careers and have found themselves teaming up many times since. From helping Dagger with family issues, to teaming up to defeat the Super Villain Carnage, Spider-Man and Cloak and Dagger continue to work together, and they are slowly realizing that that might not be such a bad thing.

MAIN ENEMIES

For a guy who is just trying to pay the bills and lead a modest life, Peter Parker has amassed one of the largest groups of enemies of any Super Hero. While Spider-Man is always trying to do the right thing, the criminals he comes into conflict with don't appreciate his actions, and tend to hold quite a grudge against the wall-crawler.

GREEN GOBLIN

There is probably no foe in Spider-Man's life that has struck as close to home as Norman Osborn, the original Green Goblin. He was responsible for the death of Peter Parker's longtime girlfriend, Gwen Stacy, and also corrupted his own son Harry's mind through verbal abuse, forging him into his goblin successor. Certifiably insane, but with a seemingly inexhaustable bank account and a horde of fanatical followers, the Green Goblin is one of the most powerful and dangerous men on the planet. Unfortunately for Peter Parker, it is Norman Osborn's avowed intention to destroy his wall-crawling archenemy, Spider-Man.

SANDMAN

One of the most powerful villains on Spidey's enemy list, the Sandman isn't quite as corrupt as many of the other rogues the wall-crawler battles against. Sandman has tried to reform himself, and he was even a reserve member of the Avengers at one point. Despite his attempts to change, he always falls back into his criminal ways in the end.

VULTURE

An elderly engineer with a brilliant mind, Adrian Toomes turned to a life of crime when he created a flying suit that gave him superior strength to any man half his age. As the Vulture, Toomes is corrupt and untrustworthy, and he has been known to betray other villains foolish enough to ally themselves with him. The activities of this hardened old bird are a cautionary tale for the equally gifted Peter Parker.

DOCTOR OCTOPUS

While there is certainly room for argument, Doctor Octopus just might be the greatest foe Spider-Man has ever faced. With a scientific mind that rivals that of Peter Parker, Doc Ock has challenged the web-slinger throughout Spidey's career. Between almost marrying Peter's Aunt May, carving out another criminal identity for himself as the "Master Planner," and attempting to take over all of the electronics in the entire city of Manhattan, Doctor Octopus is always brainstorming his next scheme. The thrill of the game seems to motivate Doc Ock just as much as the idea of a final victory over Spider-Man. He even saved Spider-Man's life on one occasion, just to ensure Spidey would live to fight him another day.

ELECTRO

Maxwell Dillon—the criminal known to the world as Electro—has been many things in his life: an electrical lineman, a super-powered thief, a pawn in a greater game, a voice of a political movement, and a living thunderbolt able to solidify himself into human form. But despite where his life takes him, it seems Electro will always side with the corrupt, and oppose everything Spider-Man stands for.

KRAVEN

A patient hunter who stalks his prey like a jungle cat, Kraven fought Spider-Man to prove he was the world's greatest hunter. Bested many times by Spidey, he shot and killed himself during his "last hunt." He has since reemerged by mystical means and remains in the shadows, preparing to hunt down his old foe.

VENOM

The Venom name and legacy started with a man named Eddie Brock. An unethical individual from childhood, Eddie grew up to be a lazy and untrustworthy journalist. Brock put his desire for fame and fortune above the integrity of his profession, and his lack of effort in carrying out proper research led to the downfall of his career. Blaming Spider-Man for proving his articles inaccurate, Brock's hatred attracted Spidey's former symbiote suit, and the first Venom was born out of their merging. Currently, Spidey's former bully Flash Thompson wears the symbiote suit, trying valiantly to control it's primal anger as a heroic incarnation of Venom.

MYSTERIO

Another of Spider-Man's foes to be personified by more than one criminal, Mysterio is far and away the most enigmatic of Spidey's enemies. With a vast knowledge of "movie magic" and special effects to craft a mysterious persona armed with bizarre weaponry, there is very little about Mysterio that is known for certain. Hiding behind smoke and mirrors in order to concoct elaborate traps for his prey, Mysterio has hunted Spider-Man many times, obsessed with seeking revenge for the numerous occasions that Spidey has foiled his plans.

CHAMELEON

The Chameleon is an expert in the field of espionage, a master criminal, and one of the first Super Villains Spider-Man faced. Using realistic masks or holographic projections, he is able to change his appearance at the drop of a hat. The Chameleon can be anyone at anytime in order to achieve his nefarious goals. Just by studying his subject for a few minutes, the Chameleon can master his victim's mannerisms, voice, and subtleties to such a degree that he can even fool those closest to his target.

CARNAGE

Already an unrepentant serial killer when he merged with a piece of Venom's symbiote suit, Cletus Kasady became a true monster as the Super Villain known as Carnage. Mentally imbalanced and with a sick bloodlust, Carnage has unleashed several campaigns against the innocents of New York City. He is so powerful that Spider-Man has barely been able to stop him. Even being ripped in two by the Avenger known as the Sentry wasn't enough to keep Kasady at bay, and he continues to return to Spider-Man's life to strike up his next campaign of terror.

HOBGOBLIN

Although several men have adopted the role of Hobgoblin over the years, Roderick Kingsley was the first to don the bizarre costume. While his equipment was mostly pilfered from the original Green Goblin, Norman Osborn, Kingsley was much more than a cheap imitation. He represented the very real threat of a sane goblin, a cold and calculating danger in Spider-Man's life until he was dethroned and killed by the current Hobgoblin, Phil Urich.

GREEN GOBLIN II

Harry Osborn followed in his father's destructive footsteps when he took up the role of the Green Goblin. One of the most tragic cases in Spider-Man's career, Harry is possibly Peter's best friend, despite being one of Spidey's greatest enemies. Struggling with a past drug addiction and a need to contain the inner mania that the goblin has caused him, Harry is constantly attempting to rebuild his life and be the father to his children that Norman Osborn never was to him.

KINGPIN

He is the master of organized crime, and his name fits him well. Wilson Fisk is the notorious Kingpin, and he has had a hand in the corruption of New York City for many years now. A foe of both Spider-Man and the vigilante Daredevil, the Kingpin runs a tight ship and has earned the respect of even the most hardened criminals. While his reign of crime has been interrupted from time to time by other would-be crime lords and heroes seeking to bring him to justice, Fisk has always reemerged on top. A brilliant fighter despite his size, the Kingpin isn't afraid to deal with situations personally when required. However, he is smart enough to hire assassins and other immoral employees to carry out the majority of his dirty work, ensuring his place at the top of the heap.

LIZARD

Dr. Curt Connors wanted nothing more than to regrow his missing limb and help countless others in a similar situation. Unfortunately, his experiments led to him becoming the blood-craving Lizard, a creature more animal than man. Instead of making his life and the world that much better, Curt's transformation led to the death of his son, as well as that of his own humanity and many a battle with Spidey.

SCORPION

Private detective Mac Gargan got more than he bargained for when he allowed J. Jonah Jameson to use him as a guinea pig in his campaign against Spider-Man. Transformed into the monstrous Scorpion by scientist Dr. Farley Stillwell, Mac used his new powers to strike out against Spider-Man. While he hates the wall-crawler, Mac also developed an equal loathing for Jameson when the newspaper editor attempted to distance himself from the Scorpion's criminal ways. Although briefly interrupted by his short tenure as Venom, Gargan continues his corrupt Scorpion career to this day.

HYDRO-MAN

Spider-Man made another enemy for life when he accidentally knocked Morris Bench off a cargo ship and into the ocean just as an experimental generator was being tested in the water. Transformed into a being capable of turning his body into a water-like liquid at will, Hydro-Man embarked on a criminal career and has even joined an anti-Spider-Man Super Villain group called the Sinister Syndicate.

JACKAL

By all appearances, Professor Miles Warren was just another college professor at Empire State University. A closeted genius with an obsession for his former student Gwen Stacy, Warren eventually adopted the identity of the Jackal, and concocted a revolutionary cloning process. Blaming Peter Parker for the death of Gwen, the Jackal cloned Parker several times. He even convinced Peter that he wasn't the original Spider-Man, but just a genetic copy. His plan was to populate the Earth with his clones, all the while toying with Peter's life to avenge Gwen's death.

SHOCKER

Convicted burglar Herman Schultz upped his game by inventing a sonic-projection suit using the tools available to him in a prison workshop. Sending out powerful sonic waves to break out of jail, Herman created the criminal persona of the Shocker, and has been repeatedly brought to justice by Spider-Man ever since.

RHINO

Just like his animal namesake, it's nearly impossible to stop a charging Rhino, but Spider-Man has done his best to try. Stuck in a permanent suit that gives him superstrength and nearly unbreakable skin, the Rhino has often tried to deny his criminal nature. Despite volunteering for the experiment that gave him his bizarre appearance, the Rhino has sought a way to surgically remove his costume in order to return to a normal life. He recently attempted to retire from crime, but his heart is truly in the wrong place, and his corrupt nature surfaces when he's faced with tragedy or even simple desire. The Rhino is a lifelong criminal, even if he hasn't fully accepted that fact.

OTHER ENEMIES

With years of crime-fighting under his belt, Spider-Man has amassed quite an impressive rogues gallery. Spidey's clashes with these repeat offenders have become such a part of his daily routine, that even he would be hard-pressed to list every villain that has ever attempted to end his career.

BOOMERANG

Australian Fred Myers moved to the United States to became a professional baseball player. Suspended for supposedly accepting bribes, Myers turned to crime with help from the clandestine organization Secret Empire. The group equipped him with an array of weaponized boomerangs—landing him his codename. Later becoming a freelance assassin, Myers often clashed with Spider-Man and joined up with other rogues to form the Sinister Syndicate.

GRAY GOBLIN

Norman Osborn and Gwen Stacy's illegitimate son, Gabriel Stacy suffered accelerated aging as Norman's newest project. With Norman's goblin formula flowing through his veins, Gabriel became the Gray Goblin, often attacking Spider-Man, and later took on the role of the American Son, all in an attempt to please his absent father.

MOLTEN MAN

Mark Raxton was the step-brother of Peter's longtime friend Liz Allan. He became the gilded Molten Man after an accident in which he was coated in a liquid metal derived from a meteor and developed by Spencer Smythe. With a hard frictionless skin and the ability to increase his external temperatures to over 500°F (260°C), Raxton became a formidable foe of Spidey's after turning to crime.

BEETLE

Abner Jenkins began his career in the world of Super Heroes as the Beetle, an enemy of the Human Torch. Using a technologically advanced flying suit of armor, the Beetle might have appeared cumbersome at first, but he was still a force to be reckoned with. Pursuing a life of crime led to him clashing with Spider-Man—giving the villain an arch foe that he would battle with many times as part of the Sinister Syndicate. These days, Jenkins has reformed and become a Super Hero going by the handle Mach-V.

JACK O'LANTERN

Jason Macendale debuted as the villainous Jack O'Lantern before upgrading his identity to that of a new Hobgoblin. Employing deadly flying devices, Jack O'Lantern was a haunting presence in Spidey's life, and one that several other criminals have filled since Macendale's departure from the role.

ENFORCERS

A trio of hired muscle available for the right price, the Enforcers have had a variety of employers over the years. However, it was when they were hired by the criminal known as the Big Man that they first encountered Spider-Man. Comprised of strong man Ox, the master of the lariat, Montana, and martial art expert and group leader Fancy Dan, the Enforcers often live up to their name.

SWARM

One of Spider-Man's most bizarre foes, Swarm is the living skeleton of former Nazi scientist Fritz von Meyer. If that wasn't strange enough, Swarm's skeleton is covered in an active hive of bees that respond to his every command and are a part of his very being. Originally an enemy of the short-lived Super Hero team the Champions, a clash with Spider-Man led Swarm to adopt the wall-crawler as his arch foe.

SPIDERCIDE

One of the Jackal's Peter Parker clones, Spidercide was corrupted from the start. After being released from a cloning chamber with no memories of who or what he was, the clone wandered the streets of New York before "realizing" that he was Peter Parker. With an obsessive sense of entitlement and complete control over his molecular structure, Spidercide was willing to kill anyone who would prevent him from taking his "rightful" place as Parker.

BURGLAR

He was the first true villain in Peter Parker's life. The man known only as the Burglar first met Spider-Man when he was robbing a TV studio during Spidey's short-lived television career. At that time, Peter couldn't be bothered to stop the obvious thief—he was more concerned about his own life, and assumed that the Burglar was someone else's problem. However, when that same thief re-emerged to rob the Parker home and shoot and kill Peter's Uncle Ben, Spidey would live to regret his inaction. Although he eventually brought the Burglar to justice, Spider-Man would never forgive himself for the criminal's deeds.

SPOT

Jonathan Ohnn was a scientist employed by the Kingpin—a thug who was attempting to recreate the powers of the Super Hero known as Cloak. Eventually succeeding in creating black disc-like portals to another dimension, Ohnn adopted the name of the Spot after his experiments caused his skin to be covered in those same black dots.

FAKE MR. AND MRS. PARKER

Peter Parker's parents had lived a fantastic life as spies for the CIA before they were killed in a sabotaged plane flight. Since Peter was a child when his parents died, he didn't have very many memories of them, so when they suddenly reappeared in his life, Peter couldn't believe his eyes. Claiming to have been held as political prisoners all these years, Peter's recently returned parents were eventually revealed to be life-like androids created by the villain Chameleon.

TINKERER

One of Spider-Man's earliest foes, Phineas Mason, aka the Tinkerer, is the modern equivalent of a mad scientist. Although he may not possess the most threatening of codenames, the Tinkerer is a brilliant inventor who has not only committed his own crimes, but has also built technology for many of Spidey's other foes.

TOMBSTONE

Hardened by a childhood as Harlem's only albino resident, Lonnie Lincoln became the whispering gangster Tombstone—a recurring presence in Spider-Man's life and one who nearly ruined the career of *Daily Bugle* mainstay, Joe Robertson.

TARANTULA

Armed with poisonous stingers built into his boots, Anton Miguel Rodriguez took his terrorist lifestyle as the Tarantula from South America to New York City. When his Super Villain career was initially cut short by a partnership between Spider-Man and the Punisher, the Tarantula's focus turned to revenge, as he now harbored a deep-seated hatred for the web-swinger.

SLYDE

Disgruntled former chemical engineer Jalome Beacher was fired from his job after inventing a frictionless chemical coating that he thought would revolutionize the frying pan industry. With no career to speak of, Jalome turned to crime, using the coating to skate over surfaces with ease and repel Spider-Man's webbing. Recently, Jalome's career was apparently ended when he was shot and seemingly killed by the criminal Underworld.

SILVERMANE

A Maggia crime lord obsessed with achieving immortality, Silvio Manfredi was dubbed Silvermane due to his prematurely white hair. Past his prime, Silvermane uses a cyborg body to stay mobile and increase his strength to superhuman proportions. He resents Spider-Man for trying to stop his quest.

SPEED DEMON

James Sanders has led a rather amazing life. Chosen by the galactic gamesman known as the Grandmaster to be one of his pawns in a grand power contest, Sanders was given super speed and originally adopted the identity of the Whizzer. After fighting the Avengers and then later the Super Hero team called the Defenders, Sanders wisely changed his name to Speed Demon to avoid confusion with a World War II era Super Hero. He then became a recurring enemy of Spider-Man's, joining up with the nefarious Sinister Syndicate.

SCORCHER

One of Norman Osborn's earliest operatives, the Scorcher—alias Steven Hudak—is an arsonist for hire, seeking revenge on Spidey for his time in prison. Using a sophisticated battle suit with built-in flamethrowers, Hudak commits crimes while remaining safely insulated.

HAMMERHEAD

When a Maggia gunman was attacked beneath a movie poster for *The Al Capone Mob*, his life was saved by disgraced surgeon Jonah Harrow. With a repaired skull made of steel alloy, he adopted the name Hammerhead and the persona of a 1920s era gangster—influenced by that landmark poster. Now he will let no one, not even Spidey, stand in his way.

SPIDER-SLAYER

Genius Inventor Spencer Smythe created the very first "Spider-Slayer," a device meant to end the career of Spider-Man. After Spencer's death, his mentally unbalanced son Alistair Smythe decided to carry on his father's legacy. Although his career got off to a rather rocky start, Alistair would later surpass the technology employed by the senior Smythe. He has since launched several campaigns against the wall-crawler, even upgrading his own body to that of a cyborg in order to become the so-called Ultimate Spider-Slayer.

CARRION

Originally a failed clone project of the Jackal, Carrion sought revenge for the assumed death of his master by lashing out at Spider-Man. Armed with a death-touch and the ability to turn his body immaterial, Carrion could make himself lighter than air, giving him a ghost-like quality that created quite a challenge for the web-slinger.

LOOTER

Experimentation on a meteorite caused would-be scientist Norton G. Fester to gain super-strength. Immediately turning to crime, Fester garbed himself in a purple and white costume and became the Looter. Reluctant to retire from his criminal ways, the Looter has battled both Peter Parker and Ben Reilly, always meeting with defeat in the end.

GRIZZLY

Maxwell Markham was a professional wrestler until the *Daily Bugle* ruined his career. After nursing his anger for eleven years, circumstances led Markham to meet the Super Villain called the Jackal. The Jackal gave the disgruntled wrestler an exo-skeleton bear costume and set Markham on the path to becoming the criminal known as the Grizzly, a fierce foe of Spidey's.

DEMOGOBLIN

When Jason Macendale made a deal with dark forces, he became a threatening presence as a demonic Hobgoblin. Later, when the demon half of his personality split off, it became Demogoblin, obsessed with killing perceived "sinners"— including Spidey.

WHITE DRAGON

The White Dragon's bid to be crime lord of Chinatown's underworld ended when he attracted Spider-Man's attention. Although he has used his skills in martial arts and gadgets, such as steel claws and a flame-throwing mask, in several grabs for power, the White Dragon has always failed, and eventually he became a pawn of Mr. Negative.

TIMELINE

- Peter Parker is born to parents Richard and Mary Parker.

- Mr. and Mrs. Parker die in a plane crash and are revealed to be spies for the CIA. Peter's Aunt May and Uncle Ben raise him as they would their own son.

- Peter attends Midtown High in Queens and excels at schoolwork, especially in the sciences. He fares much worse with his classmates, including Liz Allan and the bully Flash Thompson.

- While attending a seminar about radiation, Peter is bitten by a spider that was accidentally doused with radioactive rays. He slowly realizes that he has somehow inherited the proportionate strength and other natural abilities of a spider.

- Experimenting with his chemistry set at home, Peter develops his trademark web fluid and web-shooters. He also sneaks into school to create his first material Spider-Man costume.

- Spider-Man stars in a TV special. Backstage after the show, he lets a burglar escape past him without trying to stop him.

- Peter's Uncle Ben is killed during a botched robbery at his home.

- Peter changes into his Spider-Man costume, unaware that his neighbor's niece, Mary Jane Watson, has secretly witnessed his impressive transformation.

- Spider-Man tracks the killer to an abandoned warehouse and discovers that the criminal is none other than the same burglar he let get away back at the TV studio. He then vows to use his powers to help others, having learned that with great power there must also come great responsibility.

- *Daily Bugle* Publisher J. Jonah Jameson begins his public crusade against Spider-Man.

- Spidey saves the life of J. Jonah's son, astronaut John Jameson.

- Spider-Man petitions the Fantastic Four for membership, but reconsiders when he discovers that they don't receive salaries.

- Spider-Man battles and defeats the Chameleon for the first time.

- The Vulture and Spider-Man have their first airborne encounter.

- Peter Parker sells his first photo to J. Jonah Jameson in an effort to help his Aunt May with her money problems.

- Spider-Man fights the Tinkerer for the first time, and also unknowingly meets Mysterio who is disguised as an alien.

- Spidey develops his spider-signal belt projector to help instill fear into the hearts of criminals.

- Otto Octavius becomes Doctor Octopus and clashes with Spider-Man on their first meeting.

- The Sandman debuts and is defeated by Spider-Man.

- Spider-Man confronts the Fantastic Four's most notorious enemy, Doctor Doom.

- Heading to Florida on an assignment for the *Daily Bugle*, Spider-Man fights and defeats the Lizard for the first time.

- Spider-Man meets the Scorcher, unaware that the villain is bankrolled by Norman Osborn.

- Spider-Man meets Captain George Stacy and attempts to apply to the police force.

- Spidey helps the misunderstood Batwing after their first meeting.

- Peter Parker and Betty Brant begin to date after the Vulture returns to attack the *Daily Bugle*.

- Electro and Spider-Man clash for the first time, with Spider-Man emerging the victor.

- Spidey faces down the Enforcers and their leader, the Big Man.

- Spider-Man takes on the Headsman for the first time, another criminal under the employ of Norman Osborn.

- Peter Parker develops his first spider-tracer.

- Mysterio battles Spider-Man, the villain now garbed in his signature costume.

- Spider-Man battles the Green Goblin for the first time, but the villain gets away after leading Spidey into a fight with the Hulk.

- The Chameleon sets Kraven the Hunter on Spider-Man's trail, jumpstarting Kraven's new obsession.

- Doc Ock joins forces with Electro, Mysterio, the Vulture, Sandman, and Kraven to form the first incarnation of the Sinister Six.

- Spider-Man and Daredevil team up for the first time when they take on the Ringmaster and his Circus of Crime.

- Betty Brant's relationship with Peter begins to fizzle when she meets and dates Ned Leeds.

- J. Jonah Jameson funds Spidey's newest foe, the Scorpion.

- The Human Torch teams up with Spider-Man to battle another new member of Spidey's rogues gallery, the Beetle.

- Spencer Smythe introduces his first Spider-Slayer to J. Jonah Jameson.

- Spider-Man first crosses paths with the Crime-Master.

- Spider-Man witnesses the birth of the Molten Man, and is then forced to fight him.

- Peter graduates high school and learns of Liz Allan's crush on him.

- Peter enrolls at Empire State University alongside former bully Flash Thompson. There the two meet fellow classmates Harry Osborn and Gwen Stacy, as well as Professor Miles Warren.

- The Looter debuts and challenges Spider-Man.

- Spider-Man is faced with the robot menaces of Norman Osborn's old business partner, Mendel Stromm.

- The Green Goblin discovers Peter's dual identity and reveals himself as Norman Osborn. However, an electric charge grants Osborn with selective amnesia, and he forgets about their double lives for a time.

- The Rhino charges Spider-Man's way in their earliest encounter.

- After weeks of stalling, Peter Parker finally lets his Aunt May set him up with her friend's niece. Peter is floored when he meets the beautiful Mary Jane Watson and is instantly taken with her.

- The Avengers attempt to recruit Spider-Man, but a misunderstanding leads to Spidey sticking to his solo act.

- The Shocker sets his sights on Spidey for the first time, as does a new Vulture, Blackie Drago.

- The Kingpin makes his first play for control of New York's mobs.

- Spider-Man retires briefly before remembering the true inspiration behind his career: his Uncle Ben.

- Peter Parker meets the *Daily Bugle*'s voice of reason, Joe "Robbie" Robertson.

- Peter Parker and Gwen Stacy start dating more seriously.

- Peter meets Joe Robertson's politically active son, Randy.

- Silvermane crosses paths with both Spider-Man and the Lizard for the first time on his quest to regain his youth.

- The Prowler begins to haunt the New York night, originally clashing with Spider-Man.

- The villainous Kangaroo leaps into Spider-Man's life.

- Captain George Stacy is killed during Spider-Man's rooftop battle with Doc Ock. Spider-Man is mistaken for the killer.

- Gwen Stacy travels to Europe to deal with her loss and has a fling with Norman Osborn that results in the birth of illegitimate twins—a boy and a girl.

- Norman Osborn adopts the role of the Green Goblin again.

- Peter discovers Harry Osborn's drug addiction was due in part to Harry's failed relationship with Mary Jane Watson.

- Spider-Man grows two extra sets of arms for a time, truly appearing like his namesake. He then crosses paths with Morbius for the first time before being cured of his condition with the help of Dr. Curt Connors.

- The villainous Gibbon swings into Spider-Man's life, as does the would-be mafioso Hammerhead.

- The Green Goblin hurls Gwen Stacy, newly returned from London, from the top of the George Washington Bridge. She does not survive the fall.

- In a violent fight with Spider-Man, the Green Goblin accidentally impales himself with his glider in an incident Harry Osborn witnesses. Norman is believed to be dead.

- Peter seeks out Mary Jane Watson for comfort and sees another side to the so-called "party girl."

- John Jameson becomes the lycanthropic Man-Wolf, much to Spidey's chagrin.

- The third Vulture, Clifton Shallot, takes up the nefarious role.

- Professor Miles Warren emerges as the Jackal for the first time and hires the Punisher to fire his first shots into Spider-Man's life.

- Spider-Man takes the Spider-Mobile out for its maiden voyage.

- Spidey teams up with Ka-Zar to take on Stegron the Dinosaur Man for the first time.

- Doctor Octopus nearly marries Aunt May Parker.

- The Tarantula debuts and is instantly caught in Spidey's web.

- Harry Osborn adopts his father's identity as a new Green Goblin.

- The Grizzly rears his ugly head for the first time.

- Spider-Man moves into a new apartment and meets his neighbor Glory Grant, establishing a longtime friendship with her.

- Spider-Man not only meets the Jackal's clone of Gwen Stacy, but also his own clone doppelgänger. His clone escapes death only to leave Manhattan and adopt the identity of Ben Reilly.

- A new Mysterio, Danny Berkhart, attempts to play tricks on the wall-crawler's mind.

- Spider-Woman Jessica Drew makes a rather unorthodox debut.

- Will-O'-the-Wisp shines into Spider-Man's life.

- The heroic White Tiger and Spider-Man clash for the first time over a simple misunderstanding.

- Rocket Racer and Spider-Man meet for their initial fight.

- Harry Osborn's psychiatrist, Dr. Bart Hamilton, briefly takes over as the third Green Goblin until his untimely death.

- The White Dragon takes his first swipe at Spider-Man.

- Peter Parker graduates from Empire State University.

- Spider-Man meets the Jackal's just-as-evil clone, Carrion, as well as the sinister Fly.

- The Black Cat first crosses the wall-crawler's path.

- Peter enrolls in graduate schools at ESU and begins working as a teaching assistant for the science department.

- Spider-Man encounters a familiar new foe, the Iguana , as well as the former Champions' enemy, Swarm.

- Spider-Man has his first encounter with the mysterious and precognitive Madame Web.

- Hydro-Man wades into Spider-Man's life, followed swiftly by villains Jack O'Lantern, the Ringer, and Speed Demon.

- Spider-Man battles Cloak and Dagger, unaware that the two new vigilantes would soon become his uneasy allies.

- The killer-for-hire Boomerang focuses his attention on Spider-Man, becoming a longtime foe of the wall-crawler.

- Spidey discovers the hard way that nothing can stop the X-Men foe known as the Juggernaut—except for drying cement.

- Spidey teams up with the Frog-Man during the "hero's" debut.

- The villainous Vermin develops a new hatred for spiders after he battles the wall-crawler and Captain America.

- Spider-Man meets the criminal known as the White Rabbit during another embarrassing team-up with Frog-Man.

- The mysterious Hobgoblin begins his career by picking up where the Green Goblin left off.

- Peter Parker decides to drop out of graduate school.

- The Answer questions Spider-Man's abilities for the first time.

- Julia Carpenter adopts the role of the second Spider-Woman.

- Spider-Man returns from the Secret Wars on the alien planet Battleworld, wearing a new black symbiote alien costume.

- Spidey encounters several new rogues, including crime boss the Rose, the burglar Black Fox, and the bestial Puma.

- Spider-Man abandons his new black costume when he realizes it's alive.

- The Spot first dots the landscape of Spider-Man's life.

- Some time after marrying Harry Osborn, Liz Allan gives birth to Harry's first child, Norman Harry Osborn.

- Spider-Man meets bounty hunter Silver Sable for the first time when she is contracted to capture the Black Fox.

- The Sin-Eater viciously murders police Captain and Spider-Man ally, Jean DeWolff.

- Alistair Smythe, scientist Spencer Smythe's son and the future Ultimate Spider-Slayer, makes his less-than-impressive criminal debut, mistaking Mary Jane Watson for Spider-Man.

- A host of new criminals appear in the wall-crawler's life, including the slippery Slyde, and the deadly Chance and Foreigner.

- The Sinister Syndicate form to attempt to destroy their wall-crawling archenemy.

- Solo begins his war on terrorism, crossing paths with Spidey.

- Jason Macendale picks up the reigns as the new Hobgoblin after Ned Leeds is outed as the villain and killed.

- Long after Peter Parker realizes his true feelings for Mary Jane Watson, she finally accepts his marriage proposal.

- Peter is late to his wedding due to his adventures as Spider-Man and Mary Jane calls off the ceremony. The two soon rekindle their relationship, but marriage is now seemingly off the table forever.

- Kraven defeats Spider-Man during his "last hunt" and then commits suicide.

- Tombstone takes on the web-slinger for the first time.

- Eddie Brock becomes Venom and takes his anger out on Spidey.

- The hitmen team of Styx and Stone manifest in Spidey's life, as does the horrific Demogoblin.

- Spider-Man gains the cosmic powers and abilities of Captain Universe, as a cadre of villains stage their "Acts of Vengeance," employing the robotic Tri-Sentinel.

- Spidey is finally granted Avengers status as a reserve member.

- The Sinister Six reunite years after their original formation.

TIMELINE

- Cardiac suits up for the first time and meets Spider-Man.

- Serial killer Cletus Kasady bonds with a part of Venom's symbiote and first unleashes Carnage.

- Spider-Man meets his ferocious six-armed Doppelgänger during the Infinity War.

- Peter Parker discovers his parents are still alive, only to later find out they were robots created in a twisted game by the Chameleon.

- Spider-Man adopts his Spider-Armor to better deal with the threat of the New Enforcers.

- Harry Osborn seemingly dies due to complications with the Goblin Formula.

- Carnage meets the disturbed Shriek, and then instigates a killing spree in Manhattan.

- Spidey faces Kraven's son, the Grim Hunter, for the first time.

- Ben Reilly returns to New York when Aunt May slips into a coma. There he accidentally confronts a confused Peter Parker.

- Judas Traveller journeys to the Ravencroft Institute for the first of his bizarre experiments on Spider-Man's mind. He is accompanied by the Scrier.

- Ben Reilly adopts the persona of the Scarlet Spider.

- Kaine rears his ugly cloned head into Peter Parker's life.

- Mary Jane reveals to Peter that she is pregnant.

- The first female Scorpion, the villainous Scorpia, debuts.

- The Jackal returns from the seeming dead, and releases another Peter Parker clone, Spidercide.

- Aunt May revives from her coma only to seemingly die a week later.

- Phil Urich debuts as a heroic Green Goblin.

- A new female Doctor Octopus challenges the Scarlet Spider.

- Peter Parker officially retires from his career as Spider-Man, allowing Ben Reilly to fill the role. Ben changes Spidey's familiar costume to better suit his style, and even dyes his hair blond.

- Mary Jane gives birth to a daughter, only to have the baby stolen from her and presumed dead.

- A very much alive original Green Goblin is revealed to be the manipulator behind the Jackal and the entire Clone Saga.

- Ben Reilly makes the ultimate sacrifice to save Peter Parker from the Green Goblin. In dying, Reilly is truly confirmed to be the clone, and Parker the original.

- Peter Parker returns in full to the role of Spider-Man.

- Spider-Man meets Kraven's other son and inheritor of his moniker, Alyosha.

- Spider-Man suffers an "identity crisis" of sorts, creating four new Super Hero personas for himself.

- Aunt May is revealed to be alive—her death a masquerade orchestrated by the Green Goblin.

- Mattie Franklin, foster daughter of J. Jonah Jameson, takes on the role of the new Spider-Woman.

- Spider-Man meets Ezekiel and begins a long journey into a possible new theory behind his spider powers.

- Peter Parker embarks on a new career as a high school teacher at his old alma mater.

- Spider-Man meets the mysterious Morlun and is nearly killed in the process.

- Aunt May discovers Peter's double life, and is surprisingly accepting.

- The illegitimate children of Gwen Stacy and Norman Osborn appear in Spidey's life, as does the threat of the Gray Goblin.

- The spider-themed young heroine Araña debuts.

- Spider-Man gains organic web-shooters as a result of a confrontation with a giant spider creature called the Queen.

- Mac Gargan, formerly known as the Scorpion, becomes the new Venom after Eddie Brock auctions the symbiote off.

- Carnage gives birth to a symbiote offspring that bonds with police officer Patrick Mulligan and becomes the heroic Toxin.

- Captain America recruits Spider-Man for the New Avengers.

- The young Carmilla Black becomes the new Scorpion and goes to work for S.H.I.E.L.D.

- In a final battle with Morlun, Spider-Man is killed and reborn with enhanced powers and spike-like stingers housed in his forearms.

- Fellow Avenger Iron Man, billionaire Tony Stark, becomes Peter's mentor and designs him a hi-tech Iron Spider costume.

- Peter reveals his true identity to the world in support of Tony Stark and the Superhuman Registration Act: a law requiring all costumed heroes to register their identities with the government.

- The Super Hero Civil War breaks out over the Registration Act. Spider-Man originally sides with Iron Man and the law. However, he soon changes his allegiances after witnessing the horrors of war, and joins Captain America's group of underground rebels.

- Norman Osborn is promoted to head of the government operatives group called the Thunderbolts.

- Aunt May is shot and lies on her deathbed, forcing Spider-Man to make a deal with the devil Mephisto, costing the hero his relationship with Mary Jane Watson.

- As a favor to Spider-Man, Doctor Strange arranges it so no one remembers the wall-crawler's secret identity, save for Mary Jane.

- A Brand New Day begins in Spider-Man's life as he meets a new circle of friends including Vin Gonzales, Carlie Cooper, Lily Hollister, and a newly returned Harry Osborn.

- The mysterious heroine Jackpot debuts in New York City, as do villains Overdrive and Mr. Negative.

- The *Bugle* is bought out by Dexter Bennett, and renamed the *DB*.

- Lily Hollister secretly dons the identity of the goblin-like Menace to aid in her father, William Hollister's, mayoral campaign.

- Spider-Man meets new villains Freak, Screwball, Paper Doll, and Kraven's daughter Ana.

- Eddie Brock becomes Anti-Venom after an encounter with Mr. Negative and Venom.

- Peter meets energetic reporter Norah Winters when working at the recently established newspaper *Front Line*.

- Norman Osborn helps stop the "Secret Invasion" by the alien race known as the Skrulls. He is promoted to head of the organization formerly called S.H.I.E.L.D., renaming it H.A.M.M.E.R.

- Spider-Man meets J. Jonah Jameson Sr., and the elder Jameson soon begins to court Aunt May.

- Jackpot Alana Jobson dies of an overdose, leading to her friend Sara Ehret reclaiming the heroine's mantle.

- J. Jonah Jameson is elected Mayor of New York City.

- Spider-Man faces a new Vulture who preys on weak criminals.

- Norman Osborn takes on the public persona of the Iron Patriot, and creates his own Dark Avengers, convincing the public that Venom Mac Gargan is Spider-Man. He then attempts to get his son to take on the Super Hero role of the American Son.

- Spider-Man makes a few new enemies: the Raptor, a second Rhino, and a new Rose.

- Spider-Man joins two different branches of the Avengers after Norman Osborn is dethroned and the Superhuman Registration Act is repealed.

- The Gray Goblin assumes the role of the new American Son.

- Kraven is resurrected by his surviving family during their Grim Hunt for Spider-Man—a game that causes the death of the original Madame Web and Mattie Franklin, as well as Kraven's two sons.

- Arachne takes on the role of the new Madame Web and Araña reluctantly adopts the name of Spider-Girl.

- Lily Hollister gives birth to Harry Osborn's second son, Stanley.

- After toying with the idea, Peter Parker and Carlie Cooper finally commit to a serious relationship with one another.

- Peter takes a lucrative job as a member of the inner think tank of the innovative Horizon Labs.

- Spider-Man designs a new stealth suit to take on the newest incarnation of the Hobgoblin—a corrupted Phil Urich.

- J. Jonah Jameson's wife Marla is murdered by the Spider-Slayer.

- After a war injury leaves him a paraplegic, Flash Thompson accepts the role as the new heroic Venom.

- Spider-Man loses his spider-sense and adopts a bulletproof costume to compensate for the power downgrade.

- After the Human Torch dies, Spider-Man accepts an invitation to join the Future Foundation and dons a new costume.

- Carnage's symbiote gives birth to another spawn, which bonds with Dr. Tanis Nieves and names itself Scorn.

- The new Madame Web warns of the coming of Spider-Island.

TIMELINE

It is still perhaps the most important decade in Spider-Man's comic book career. The 1960s not only saw the birth of the fabled wall-crawler himself, but they also ushered in one of the greatest rogues galleries in the history of comic books.

THE
1960s

Stan Lee was showing the competition how it was done. While DC Comics was the company to beat with such icons as Superman, Batman, and the newly established Justice League of America, Lee and Marvel had just proven themselves to be true innovators. First with the Fantastic Four, and then with Spider-Man and a host of other new heroes, Lee was adding a new dimension to the Super Hero makeup. Unlike the united heroes of the Justice League, the Fantastic Four members argued among themselves like a real family. Unlike the confident Superman and Batman, Spider-Man had doubts, anxieties, and real-world problems. Along with his amazing artistic partners, Stan Lee had found a way to breathe new life into the Super Hero set, and Spider-Man was at the center of the movement.

But not content to rest on his laurels, Lee knew that every good hero needs a whole hoard of evil villains to help shape him and build his legend. With the creation of dozens of top tier Spidey foes, from the Green Goblin and Doctor Octopus to *Daily Bugle* publisher J. Jonah Jameson, Lee secured the future of his foremost creation as an American icon.

March 1963

THE AMAZING SPIDER-MAN #1

"We cannot allow that masked menace to take the law into his own hands! He is a bad influence on our youngsters!"

J. JONAH JAMESON

EDITOR-IN-CHIEF
Stan Lee

COVER ARTISTS
Jack Kirby and Steve Ditko

WRITER
Stan Lee

PENCILER
Steve Ditko

INKER
Steve Ditko

LETTERERS
Johnny Dee
and John Duffi

MAIN CHARACTERS: Spider-Man; Aunt May Parker; J. Jonah Jameson; John Jameson; the Chameleon; Mr. Fantastic; Invisible Girl; the Human Torch; the Thing
MAIN SUPPORTING CHARACTERS: The Burglar; Professor Newton
MAIN LOCATIONS: The Parker residence; unnamed rocket launch site; the Baxter Building; unnamed defence installation, New York City; the Chameleon's secret hideout; unnamed waterfront, New York City

BACKGROUND

Picking up right where they left off in *Amazing Fantasy* #15 (August 1962), writer-editor Stan Lee and artist Steve Ditko took Spider-Man out for another web-spin in the debut issue of the character's ongoing comic book series, *The Amazing Spider-Man*. The debut issue featured two self-contained stories. The lead story was a fairly standard adventure, and while it boasted the first appearance of the recurring thorn in Peter Parker's side, J. Jonah Jameson, it wasn't the reason most readers were buying the issue.

That honor fell to the second story, featuring the first-ever meeting of Spider-Man and the famous Fantastic Four. Already a hit in Stan Lee's new era of Marvel Comics, the Fantastic Four were also featured on the cover as a clever marketing strategy. Not only did their appearance solidify the fact that Spider-Man operated in the shared Marvel Universe, but it also succeeded in coaxing some of the Fantastic Four's fans to give Spider-Man a try. And if the resultant success of *The Amazing Spider-Man* is any indication, most of those fans stuck around for the long haul.

"I came up here to join up with you!
I wanna be a member of
the **Fantastic Four!**"

SPIDER-MAN

THE STORIES

Spider-Man saves the life of astronaut John Jameson, despite the smear campaign against the hero, orchestrated by John's father, J. Jonah Jameson. In the second story, Spidey meets the Fantastic Four for the first time before battling the enigmatic Chameleon.

Being Spider-Man was quickly proving more trouble than Peter Parker had imagined. Not only could Spider-Man not cash the checks he made for his TV appearances (he would need identification to do so), but also the publisher of the *Daily Bugle*, J. Jonah Jameson, was actively delivering lectures all over town about the supposed threat Spider-Man posed to the citizens of his city (**1**). While many believed Jameson's campaign was merely a publicity stunt to draw in new readers and promote his son, astronaut John Jameson, Spider-Man nevertheless saw his career in showbiz take a brutal nosedive.

However, while attending the launch of John Jameson's space shuttle (**2**), Peter stood by in witness as John lost control of the craft due to a technical malfunction. Realizing what had happened, the officials at ground control tried, unsuccessfully, to think of a way to save the space shuttle (**3**). But Peter Parker was no longer content to sit idly by when faced with the opportunity to help others in need. Peter changed swiftly into his Spider-Man costume (**4**), and commandeering a plane and its pilot from a nearby airfield, used a web-line to swing aboard the capsule (**5**). He attached a space guidance unit he'd been given by a military official to the capsule (**6**). With Spider-Man's help, John landed the craft safely, and Peter returned home, only to discover that J. Jonah Jameson had increased his anti-Spider-Man agenda, claiming the web-slinger had deliberately put John's mission in harm's way in order to rescue him in a public arena (**7**). It seemed Spider-Man had had his first run in with the all too infamous "Parker luck."

In the issue's second feature, Peter Parker was no closer to helping his poor aunt pay her bills. But there were other heroes who didn't seem to share Peter's financial woes. Spider-Man headed to the world-famous Baxter Building in an attempt to meet and join the fabled Fantastic Four.

Of course, one doesn't just waltz into the Fantastic Four's home and say "hello." In order to meet with the heroes, Spider-Man broke into their headquarters, bypassing their security safeguards (**8**). An alarm sounded and the Fantastic Four saw that it was Spider-Man who was breaking in (**9**). They weren't pleased that a "teenage show-off" thought he could take them by surprise. A violent clash ensued (**10**), until Spider-Man was able to plead his case. He had wanted to prove to them that he had what it takes to be a member of the Fantastic Four. Spidey's mission had been made in vain, however, as the team informed him that they didn't receive a salary for their heroics.

Meanwhile, the mysterious master of disguise and Super Villain known as the Chameleon (**11**) decided to capitalize on Spider-Man's outlaw status with the press. After devising his own artificial web-shooting gun, the Chameleon stole prized missile plans from a government installation, while wearing a replica of Spider-Man's costume (**12**). Despite the clever frame-up, Spider-Man managed to track the villain to the waterfront, and was just about to return him to the authorities (**13**) when the Chameleon disappeared. Spidey used his spider-sense to detect that the villain was disguised as one of the cops (**14**), but the real police officers refused to believe that Spider-Man wasn't the criminal. Spider-Man fled in anger, leaving the police officers to figure it out. Spider-Man may have saved the day, but he wished he had never got his superpowers. He was a loner with a tarnished reputation and a laughable bank balance.

A LIFE OF CRIME

Driven insane and more power-hungry than ever by the explosion in his lab, Norman Osborn decided to increase his personal fortune by turning to crime. He hired and outfitted costumed Super Villains like the Scorcher and the Headsman. But when these thieves were defeated by Spider-Man, Norman decided to take matters into his own hands. He used his company's chemical discoveries to assemble a personal armory and designed a costume for himself. All he needed was the right mask—a face to present to the world. He chose the face of the Green Goblin.

Norman based his grotesque green costume and mask on a green goblin monster from a childhood nightmare.

The Green Goblin keeps a bizarre variety of gas, smoke, and incendiary grenades in his "bag of tricks."

KEY DATA

FIRST APPEARANCE: *The Amazing Spider-Man* #14 (July 1964)

REAL NAME: Norman Osborn

AFFILIATIONS: The Sinister Twelve, the Thunderbolts, the Cabal, H.A.M.M.E.R., Dark Avengers

POWERS/ABILITIES: The Goblin Formula endows Norman Osborn with enhanced intelligence, strength, reflexes, agility, speed, and endurance, and a regenerative healing ability. He possesses a vast array of deadly, high-tech weapons, including grenade-like pumpkin bombs and his flying Goblin-Glider. He wears a chain mail tunic for extra protection in battle.

The Goblin's signature weapons are his deadly pumpkin bombs, shaped as miniature Jack-O'-Lanterns.

Osborn created his ingenious Goblin-Glider, which travels at speeds of 90 mph (140 kph). Originally he flew on a rocket-like "broomstick," but soon traded that in for the razor-wings and better maneuverability of his Glider.

GREEN GOBLIN

To say Norman Osborn is simply insane is to do the criminal a great injustice. Arguably Spider-Man's most dangerous enemy, the Green Goblin has cheated death to continue his quest for power and his never-ending campaign against the web-slinger.

When Norman attempted to recreate a serum to enhance his strength and intelligence, he thought it had failed when it bubbled and exploded in his face.

ORIGIN

Norman Osborn was just a child when he first became obsessed with acquiring wealth and power. His father, Amberson Osborn, was an inventor whose business failed, and he often took out his rage on his young son. Norman realized that he couldn't depend on his father for financial security, so he began working after school and saving every cent that he earned. Driven and dedicated, Norman studied chemistry, business administration, and electrical engineering in college. He became good friends with one of his teachers, Professor Mendel Stromm, and they formed a business partnership. Since Norman had put up the bulk of the financing, they called their company Osborn Chemical. Norman married his college sweetheart and they had a son, Harry, a few years later, but his wife became ill and died. After her death, Norman buried himself in his work and rarely had time for young Harry. Norman eventually learned that his business partner had embezzled money from their company so he had Stromm arrested and assumed complete control of the company. While going through Stromm's notes, Norman learned of a chemical formula that could increase a person's strength and intelligence, so he tried to recreate the experiment. But unaware that his angry son had switched a few of his chemicals, the solution turned green and exploded. After he was released from hospital following the explosion, Norman realized that the formula had worked—he was stronger and smarter than ever.

"You **see**, Parker? I always knew I could defeat you anytime I **wanted**..."

Green Goblin

Originally, the Goblin simply wanted to establish his criminal reputation by killing Spider-Man. But with each defeat, he became more obsessed with conquering the wall-crawler.

Although Norman Osborn is a respected businessman and government official, he can't help but relapse into his Goblin persona to continue his crazed pursuit of Spider-Man.

The Green Goblin once learned Spider-Man's secret identity by exposing him to a gas that weakened his spider-sense. However, Spidey knocked the villain into a mass of live electrical wires and gave Osborn amnesia.

While the Goblin Formula increases its user's physical strength and even his intelligence, it also costs him his sanity. However, that was a small price to pay for a man as ruthless as Norman Osborn.

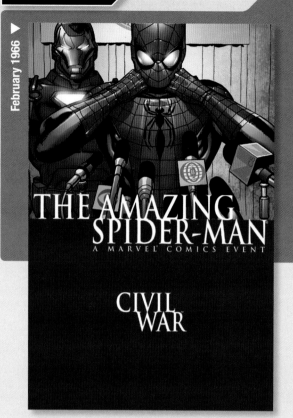

February 1966 ▲

THE AMAZING SPIDER-MAN
A MARVEL COMICS EVENT

CIVIL WAR

THE AMAZING SPIDER-MAN #33

"But, I can't give up! I must keep trying! I must!!"

SPIDER-MAN

EDITOR-IN-CHIEF
Stan Lee

COVER ARTISTS
Jack Kirby and
Steve Ditko

WRITER
Stan Lee

PENCILER
Steve Ditko

INKER
Steve Ditko

LETTERER
Art Simek

MAIN CHARACTERS: Spider-Man; Aunt May Parker; Dr. Curt Connors; Dr. Octopus; J. Jonah Jameson; Betty Brant
MAIN SUPPORTING CHARACTERS: Fredrick Foswell; Bennett Brant; Kraven (cameo)
MAIN LOCATIONS: A hospital, New York; Dr. Connor's lab; Dr. Octopus's underwater hideout; the *Daily Bugle* office; various New York City streets

BACKGROUND

While it might not rival the cliffhangers of TV shows, such as the "Who shot J.R.?" conundrum in *Dallas*, or the mysteries surrounding the premise of the TV hit *Lost*, back in 1965, Spider-Man fans had their own ongoing mystery to ponder. Just who was the enigmatic Master Planner?

A seemingly new player trying his hand at the criminal underworld, the Master Planner emerged in *The Amazing Spider-Man* #31, stationed in an exotic underwater hideout that was staffed with hundreds of minions clad in purple uniforms. While Spidey fans only had to wait until issue #32 to find that the Master Planner was in fact Spider-Man's old foe, Dr. Octopus, by then, the readers were hooked in a multi-part storyline that held the life of Peter Parker's elderly Aunt May in the balance.

However, this wasn't the first time Lee and company had used a mystery to keep readers coming back month after month. Perhaps their most successful attempt had been the question of the secret identity of the recurring villain Green Goblin. The use of these tantalizing subplots only added to the enjoyment of the title, and created a more serialized feel for the issues than the stand-alone comics created by some of Marvel's competitors.

"I've done the best I could, Aunt May!" Now there's nothing left, but prayer–!"

SPIDER-MAN

THE STORY

Pinned by a seemingly impossible weight, and with his beloved Aunt May's life depending upon his escape, Spider-Man must find the strength to battle his way to safety.

They called the serum ISO-36. An experimental concoction developed on the West Coast, it was reported to help significantly in alleviating radiation poisoning. But to Peter Parker, it was more than just a scientific curiosity. To Peter Parker, ISO-36 was his Aunt May's last hope (**1**).

Weeks earlier, in an effort to help the ailing May, Peter had eagerly volunteered his own blood for a transfusion. At the time, May had recovered completely, but after a while, the radiation in Spider-Man's blood had weakened her, until she was once again hospitalized and at death's door. After visiting the lab of the sometime Lizard, Dr. Curt Connors, Spider-Man learned of ISO-36's existence, and pawned all of his science equipment in order to afford its high cost. Connors arranged for a shipment of the serum from the other side of the country, but neither he nor Peter had any idea that a familiar face from Spider-Man's past had his eye on the experimental formula.

Under the guise of the Master Planner, Dr. Octopus had his men pilfer the serum when it arrived in New York, and deliver it to his secret underwater headquarters. There, Doc Ock planned on continuing his research, hoping to master radiation in an effort to gain even more power. Spider-Man tracked the villain back to his headquarters, but in a violent scuffle, found himself trapped under a pile of heavy machinery, with the canister of ISO-36 just out of his reach, and water slowly leaking in from the damaged structure of the underwater lair (**2**).

Channeling all of his inner strength, and thinking of the life of his Aunt May, and that of his beloved Uncle Ben before her, Spider-Man managed the impossible. Little by little, he began to rise to his feet, lifting the wreckage higher and higher until he was finally free (**3**). Stumbling through the wet chamber with fairly severe injuries and the canister of ISO-36 clasped tightly to his chest (**4**), Spider-Man then fought his way through a flash flood in the underwater chamber, complete with a few of Dr. Octopus's men garbed in scuba gear. Finally emerging into a dry chamber of the headquarters, Spidey was then faced with a dozen more of the villainous henchmen (**5**), before he escaped to the laboratory of Dr. Curt Connors.

Spider-Man worked with Dr. Connors to test the serum (**6**). While Dr. Connors wasn't looking, Spider-Man took a sample of his own radioactive blood. He tested the serum on the sample (**7**), not telling the doctor where or whom it came from. Spider-Man knew that if the serum worked on his own radioactive blood, it should work on his aunt, too. All that remained was to deliver the serum to the hospital, and hope that it would be enough to cure his aunt.

The next two hours of anxious waiting went by in a hazy blur for Peter Parker. Spider-Man returned to the warehouse to discover the Master Planner's gang were still out cold (**8**). He alerted the police and snapped pictures of the arrest of the henchmen (**9**). He delivered them to the *Daily Bugle* and into the ecstatic hands of its publisher, J. Jonah Jameson (**10**).

But the time did indeed pass, and soon enough Peter was at the hospital by his aunt's side. The doctors told Peter that Spider-Man's serum had stopped the blood deterioration, and that his dear aunt was going to pull through. Aunt May woke briefly, squeezed Peter's hand, and even smiled (**11**). Spider-Man had won this battle. While baffled doctors pondered how Spider-Man fitted into this all, Peter Parker headed home to finally allow himself some much needed rest.

Spidey was growing up. In the tumultuous 1970s, the hero dealt with the death of loved ones and watched a friend fall victim to a drug addiction. Despite the controversy, Spidey remained as popular as ever, even earning a new monthly title in *Peter Parker: The Spectacular Spider-Man.*

THE
1970s

It was time for Spider-Man to sink or swim. In 1971, for the first time in his fictional life, the web-slinger would be forced to make his way in the Marvel Universe without the direct help of writer Stan Lee. After taking Peter Parker to the historic 100th issue of *The Amazing Spider-Man* (an issue that featured Spidey gaining four extra arms), Lee thought it best to step out from behind the writer's desk to pursue other avenues. And while he'd return to pen Spidey's adventures once or twice in the future, Lee was no longer charting the course of the hero's life.

This wasn't the first time that the creative team behind Spider-Man had shifted. Legendary artist Steve Ditko had left the title after issue #38 in 1966, and this had made way for the similarly renowned artwork of John Romita. Artist extraordinaire John Buscema had penciled a handful of issues, and the amazing Gil Kane had even taken on the task of drawing the wall-crawler a few times. But Lee leaving the book was the title's ultimate test, and one it passed with flying colors. With the groundbreaking work of future writers like Gerry Conway, *The Amazing Spider-Man* kept earning its titular adjective issue after issue.

KEY DATA

FIRST APPEARANCE: *The Amazing Spider-Man* #25 (June 1965)

ALIAS: None

AFFILIATIONS: None

PERSONALITY TRAITS: Mary Jane is a source for calm and reason in Peter Parker's otherwise chaotic life. Although she has no special powers, she is intelligent and resourceful in times of danger, often displaying exemplary courage and tenacity. She possesses a wide range of acting skills and is trained in self-defense.

Mary Jane's career as a model has meant that her clothes are always at the height of fashion. Even her casual wear boasts impressive name brands.

Due to her tough childhood, Mary Jane is great at masking her feelings. It's a talent that has been useful for her acting career and for making up excuses for Peter's activities.

SPIDER-MAN'S GIRLFRIEND

It wasn't until Peter Parker and Mary Jane Watson began getting serious about one another that Mary Jane realized the high price that accompanied being in a relationship with Spider-Man. Danger is always present in the wall-crawler's life, and if MJ wasn't worrying about Peter coming home safely, she was worrying about her own well-being. Over the years, Mary Jane has been attacked by the likes of Tombstone and the second incarnation of the Green Goblin. However, the greatest impact on her was made by Venom. When the villain first arrived on the scene, he went straight to Mary Jane and Peter's apartment. There he confronted the model and asked her about Peter's whereabouts. MJ was so scared by Venom's visit that she persuaded Peter to move apartments.

During her relationship with Peter, Mary Jane was often the breadwinner of the household, having a much more successful career.

MARY JANE

On the surface, Mary Jane Watson is the complete opposite of Peter Parker. Seemingly merely a fun-loving, carefree party girl with a constant smile on her face, Mary Jane proves that looks can be deceiving. There is far more to MJ than just a pretty face.

ORIGIN

Mary Jane is the daughter of Philip and Madeline Watson. Her mother was a drama student, while her father majored in American literature and wanted to be a writer. The two married as soon as they graduated from college. But as his dreams of becoming a writer faltered, Philip turned on his family, verbally abusing them and blaming them for his inability to concentrate. The relationship deteriorated to the extent that Madeline took their young children, Gayle and Mary Jane, and left Philip.

Life did not get any easier for the Watson family. Gayle married her high-school sweetheart Timothy Byrnes right after graduation. Timmy planned to be a lawyer, but the couple became pregnant. Unable to cope with the pressures of law school, and with yet another child on the way, Timmy deserted Gayle. Disaster struck again, when Mary Jane's mother died just before the birth of Gayle's second child. Gayle turned to her sister, hoping for support. But Mary Jane wasn't willing to give up her dream of becoming an actress to help her sister. Instead, she left to stay with her favorite aunt, Anna Watson, who was living in Forest Hills. During her time there, Aunt Anna introduced Mary Jane to a young man that would change her life forever. A young man named Peter Parker.

Though reluctant to let his aunt set him up on a date, when Peter finally met MJ, he couldn't believe how beautiful she was.

Mary Jane first discovered Peter's dual identity when she saw Spider-Man crawl out of Peter's bedroom on the night that Peter's Uncle Ben died. However it took her years before she revealed to Peter that she knew.

"Face it, Tiger... You just hit the jackpot!"

Mary Jane

During the time Mary Jane lived with Peter, she was kidnapped by Green Goblin Harry Osborn. Although Mary Jane was terrified at first, Harry didn't want to harm his friend.

A popular model and former star of the soap opera *Secret Hospital*, Mary Jane is used to a life of glitz and glamour.

Mary Jane has had many admirers, but none were more obsessive or dangerous than her former landlord Jonathan Caesar, who even attempted to kidnap her at one point.

While they are no longer a couple, Mary Jane and Peter still have strong feelings for each other. MJ remains a true friend to Peter as one of the few people to know about his double life.

THE DEATH OF THE STACYS

Beautiful science undergrad Gwen Stacy was the first woman who truly captured the heart of Peter Parker. As their relationship blossomed, Peter grew to love her more than any of the women he had dated in the past, and wanted to spend the rest of his life with her. But fate had other plans for them.

THE BEGINNING OF THE END

After dating for some time, Gwen and Peter were becoming more serious about each other and Peter was introduced to Gwen's father, retired police captain George Stacy. Stacy was kind to Peter, and what's more, he appeared to be a Spider-Man supporter. It seemed that, like Peter, George was a hero at heart. George's heroism was proven during a rooftop battle between Spider-Man and Doctor Octopus. When stone debris hurtled toward an innocent child, George leapt into action. He put himself in harm's way and saved the child's life.

Horrified at what had happened, Spider-Man pulled his girlfriend's father from the rubble. George Stacy knew he was dying and deduced Spider-Man's secret identity. As he died in Peter's arms, he begged Peter to watch over Gwen and take care of her. Even though Captain Stacy accepted his fate, Peter always blamed himself for the man's death.

THE RETURN OF THE GREEN GOBLIN

Some time after George Stacy's death, trouble started to brew for Peter's friends. Harry Osborn began taking drugs, and the stress of dealing with this pushed his father, Norman, into insanity, leading to him resuming his role as the Green Goblin. Norman blamed Peter for Harry's condition and set out to take revenge by abducting Peter's girlfriend, Gwen Stacy.

CALLING CARD

When Spidey returned to his apartment, the place was in a shambles and a Jack-O'Lantern, the Green Goblin's trademark weapon, rested on Gwen's purse. Realizing she had been kidnapped, Spider-Man used his spider-sense to track the Green Goblin to the top of the George Washington Bridge.

Norman Osborn had kidnapped Gwen by sneaking up on her from behind while she was distracted, worrying about the drug-addled condition of his son, Harry.

> "YOU KILLED THE WOMAN I LOVE— AND FOR THAT, YOU'RE GOING TO DIE!"
> SPIDER-MAN

During a furious battle with the wall-crawler atop the George Washington Bridge, the Goblin hurled Gwen over the side. Spider-Man shot out a web-line that caught the falling Gwen, but when he pulled her up, he was horrified to discover that she was already dead. While Spidey grieved, the Goblin escaped.

REVENGE

Spider-Man set out to find the Green Goblin and end his career once and for all. But, as much as he hated the Goblin, Spidey knew he couldn't take the life of another human being. He bested Osborn, and was about to take him captive when the villain mentally ordered his glider to impale Spider-Man. Warned by his spider-sense, Spidey ducked at the last moment. The glider impaled Osborn, killing him instantly—or so it seemed…

October 1975

THE AMAZING SPIDER-MAN #149

*"... the day I can't tell if I'm really **me**—is the day I hang up my web-shooters forever!"*

SPIDER-MAN (OR POSSIBLY HIS CLONE...)

EDITOR
Marv Wolfman

COVER ARTIST
Gil Kane

WRITER
Gerry Conway

PENCILER
Ross Andru

INKER
Mike Esposito

COLORIST
Janice Cohen

LETTERER
Annette Kawecki

MAIN CHARACTERS: Spider-Man; the Jackal; Gwen Stacy's clone; Spider-Man's clone

MAIN SUPPORTING CHARACTERS: Ned Leeds; the Tarantula; Anthony Serba; Mary Jane Watson; Joe Robertson; J. Jonah Jameson; Betty Brant

MAIN LOCATIONS: The Brooklyn Bridge; an abandoned tenement in lower Manhattan; Empire State University campus; the Jackal's laboratory; the *Daily Bugle* office; Shea Stadium; an unnamed cemetery, Queens; Peter Parker's apartment

BACKGROUND

It was the start of the most controversial storyline in the entire history of Spider-Man. The seeds planted in this 1975 multi-part storyline would slowly grow into the largest crossover ever to shake-up the Spidey universe—in the 1990s Clone Saga epic.

The writer Gerry Conway was no stranger to controversy. After all, just a few years earlier he had penned the death of Spider-Man's longtime love interest, Gwen Stacy, at the hands of the Green Goblin. And when Gwen seemingly returned in the months preceeding issue #149, fans were unprepared to learn she was merely a clone created by Peter Parker's teacher, Professor Miles Warren. Fans were even more shocked to learn that Warren was in fact the Super Villain named the Jackal, who had been causing most of Peter Parker's recent problems.

But no matter what the surprises in the past, fans would not be ready for the Jackal's newest clone, who leapt onto the pages of *The Amazing Spider-Man* #149. Just as they would be caught off guard nearly twenty years later when that same clone returned.

THE STORY

Faced with a bizarre challenge set by the insane Jackal, Spider-Man must defeat his own clone in order to rescue an innocent life.

There was no shortage of excitement in Spider-Man's world. He had recently faced down the new threat of the Grizzly, wrecked his Spider-Mobile due to the machinations of Mysterio, and learned of a new Super Villain out to kill him named the Jackal. And while Spider-Man's life was complicated, it couldn't hold a candle to Peter Parker's. Because just as Peter and Mary Jane Watson seemed to be taking their relationship to the next level, a familiar face popped back into Peter's life—the face of Gwen Stacy, Peter's former girlfriend whom he'd thought long dead.

Alongside Gwen's unexplained return came Peter's feelings for her. But before he could really process them, he found himself in a violent conflict with the Jackal and his accomplice, the Tarantula. While Spider-Man managed to defeat the Tarantula, the Jackal succeeded in subduing the web-crawler with his drug-tipped claws. With Spider-Man at his mercy, the Jackal revealed himself as Peter Parker's old college biology teacher, Professor Miles Warren.

While strapped to a table in the basement of an abandoned tenement building in lower Manhattan, Spider-Man had no choice but to listen to the mad ramblings of his former teacher (**1**). Even after the hero broke free of his bonds and engaged the Jackal in a brutal physical confrontation (**2**), the villain was determined to tell his bizarre story.

According to the Jackal, while he was teaching Peter's class, he'd developed quite an infatuation with Gwen Stacy. When the young girl died at the hands of the Green Goblin, Professor Warren had blamed Spider-Man for her death. He used tissue samples he had acquired from a classroom study to clone the young woman. In the process, Warren killed his lab assistant Anthony Serba, when Serba discovered what the Professor was up to. It was this traumatic event that caused Warren to truly plunge into insanity (**3**), and to develop the alter ego and split personality of the Jackal. He brought Gwen Stacey's doppelgänger to life (**4**) and vowed to defeat Spider-Man.

After relaying his tale, the Jackal then escaped, telling Spider-Man that if he ever wanted to see Gwen Stacy again, he would have to head to Shea Stadium at midnight that night. Forced to follow the madman's directions, Spider-Man arrived at the baseball field (**5**) only to once again be drugged by the villain. And when he awoke this time, Spider-Man was shocked to discover that he wasn't alone. Lying on the ground next to him was his clone, an exact double of Peter Parker, even down to the Spider-Man costume he wore.

The Jackal told the web-crawlers that only the real Peter Parker would be able to release his captive, Ned Leeds. With a ticking time bomb waiting to explode above the head of Ned, Spider-Man and his clone battled (**6**). But they realized the folly of their actions and turned their attention to the Jackal and rescuing Ned. Meanwhile, the hypnotic spell that the Jackal had cast over Gwen Stacy's clone wore off. Calling him a murderer, Gwen caused the Jackal to realize the insanity of his plan (**7**). He released Ned into the arms of Spider-Man and his clone (**8**). But the bomb was still set to explode. While Ned Leeds and Spider-Man survived the ensuing explosion, the Jackal died instantly. Caught beneath the devastation, it seemed that Spider-Man's clone had died too (**9**).

After the smoke cleared, the Gwen Stacy clone took off to explore the world, and an exhausted Peter Parker headed home (**10**). With his spider-sense tingling, Peter opened the door. But it was a welcome surprise—Mary Jane Watson was waiting for him.

*"Someday I'm going to learn to wear **ear-plugs** when I'm fighting crime."*

SPIDER-MAN

SPIDER-WOMEN

More than one super-powered woman has taken on the mantle of Spider-Woman over the years. In total, there have been four Spider-Women (although one turned out to be the creation of an evil genius), plus one Spider-Girl.

Jessica has the ability to fire bio-electric "venom blasts" from her fingertips to stun or kill opponents.

JESSICA DREW

While Jessica Drew and Peter Parker became super-powered in different ways, Jessica has become quite a fixture in Spider-Man's world these days. As Avengers teammates, the two see quite a lot of each other, despite Jessica often being annoyed by Spidey's constant need to add wisecracks and colorful commentary to every battle. Jessica gained her spider-powers while in her mother's womb when her mother was caught in a lab accident during one of her scientist father's experiments. At a young age, Jessica was trained to be a field agent of the criminal organization Hydra. But she later turned her back on the corrupt institution and carved out a name for herself as the world's first Spider-Woman, a title she holds as an active crime-fighter to this day.

Just like Spider-Man, Jessica can adhere to most surfaces. She also possesses enhanced speed, strength, and endurance.

JULIA CARPENTER

Although she is now known as the precognitive Madame Web, Julia Carpenter started off her Super Hero career as the second Spider-Woman. Having been injected with a mysterious serum that allowed her to project super-strong psionic webs with her mind, Julia adopted a black and white uniform and set out to do her best to help society. Inspiring many others over the course of her career, Julia's costume even subconsciously influenced Spider-Man to wear a black costume of his own when he first tried on his alien symbiote suit. Julia later changed her name to Arachne before accepting the role as the new Madame Web, and she passed her black and white costume to Spider-Girl, Anya Corazon. Julia has gained many friends and allies throughout her Super Hero career, serving on various Super Hero teams including the Avengers.

ANYA CORAZON

While she never called herself Spider-Woman per se, Anya has recently taken on the role of Spider-Girl, although she was more comfortable with her original hero name, Araña. The benefactor of powers from a mystical spider cult that believed in the totemistic powers of the spider, Anya became an adventurer, making the most of the powers granted to her. Her powers have faded in and out and she lost her father to an imposter incredible Hulk, but while her life has not been without tragedy, Anya tries to keep positive, even finding time to microblog about her adventures.

MATTIE FRANKLIN

During a period when Peter Parker temporarily retired as Spider-Man, Mattie Franklin stepped up to fill his role. Gaining powers during a mystical ritual meeting called the Gathering of Five, Mattie put those abilities to good use while masquerading as the original wall-crawler. When Peter returned to his heroic career, she began going by the name Spider-Woman, until her eventual downfall. Mattie's life soon sunk so low that at one point her blood was sold on the black market as the drug Mutant Growth Hormone.

CHARLOTTE WITTER

Not all the women to adopt the name of Spider-Woman have been out to protect the world. Charlotte Witter was a tortured soul, programmed to destroy the spider-powered heroes of the world by Doctor Octopus. Witter had been a fashion designer until Octopus saw something in her and decided to kidnap her. Doc Ock used torture, starvation, and genetic experimentation to brainwash Witter into becoming his willing slave. Converted to Octopus's cause and armed with four spider-like legs, this corrupt Spider-Woman set out to prey on others with her same name. She eventually drew Spider-Man's attention after she brutally attacked fledgling heroine Mattie Franklin.

Mattie's short life came to a close when she was kidnapped by the Kraven family during their "Grim Hunt." She was stabbed in a ritualistic ceremony to raise Kraven's son, the Grim Hunter, from his grave.

Comics were growing darker, and even the lighthearted nature of Spider-Man wasn't immune to the trend. In a decade dominated by gritty violence and noir threats, Peter Parker managed to stay above it all, even if his costume did not.

THE
1980s

By the 1980s, Spider-Man's costume was iconic. The friendly wall-crawler had reached a level of comic book super-stardom usually only reserved for characters with a good 20 years of history on him. But through his hit comic, various TV spotlights, and merchandising, Spider-Man's intricate red and blue threads were known not only nationwide, but worldwide. So, Marvel decided to throw everyone for a loop and change Spidey's clothes.

In Marvel's first giant crossover blockbuster called *Marvel Super Heroes Secret Wars*, Spider-Man journeyed to a faraway planet called Battleworld, and discovered a black alien costume. He brought the suit back with him, and just like that, there was a new Spider-Man on the block.

While the alien didn't stay a permanent part of Spider-Man's wardrobe, the black look certainly did. In an era populated by comics inspired by Frank Miller's seminal gritty classic Batman: *The Dark Knight Returns* and Alan Moore's dark masterpiece *Watchmen*, it seemed only appropriate that Spider-Man should dress for the new level of disturbing threats he would face in the coming years.

January 1984

MARVEL
The AMAZING
SPIDER-MAN
60¢ 248 JAN
U.K. 25p
CAN. 75¢

IN THIS ISSUE MEET:
"THE KID WHO COLLECTS SPIDER-MAN"

THE AMAZING SPIDER-MAN #248

*"Spider-Man wants to meet **me**?!
Now I **know** I'm dreaming!"*

Timothy Harrison

EDITOR-IN-CHIEF
Jim Shooter

COVER ARTIST
John Romita Jr. and
Terry Austin

WRITER
Roger Stern

PENCILER
Ron Frenz

INKER
Terry Austin

LETTERER
Joe Rosen

COLORIST
Christie Scheele

MAIN CHARACTERS: Spider-Man; Timothy Harrison
MAIN SUPPORTING CHARACTERS: Jacob Conover; The Burglar; Aunt May Parker; Uncle Ben Parker
MAIN LOCATIONS: Slocum-Brewer Cancer Clinic; an unnamed TV studio, New York; the Parker residence; Acme warehouse, Queens, New York

BACKGROUND

By all appearances, *The Amazing Spider-Man* #248 looked like much of the other standard Super Hero fare of the time period. The cover boasted an action-packed image of a hero fighting a villain, and seemed to promise a fairly commonplace battle between good and evil. The first story of the issue delivered just what was expected as Spider-Man battled it out with Thunderball, a member of the villainous Wrecking Crew. But it was the issue's backup story that would elevate this comic book into something more memorable than the rest of the month's offerings. In fact, "The Kid Who Collects Spider-Man" would go on to be one of the most memorable and most loved stories of all time.

Influenced by the style of cartoonist and writer Will Eisner's comic book *The Spirit*, writer Roger Stern crafted a human-interest Spider-Man story in which neither Peter Parker nor his web-headed alter ego would be the focus of the tale. Instead, Stern used Spider-Man merely as a supporting character, yet still managed to throw in a shocking climax and a twist ending that fans still discuss to this day. This special story is regarded by many fans as one of the greatest Spider-Man yarns ever told.

THE STORY

Spider-Man visits his number one fan, Timothy Harrison, and makes the compassionate decision to reveal his secret identity to the young boy.

Timothy Harrison was different from most boys his age. While he enjoyed the majority of the normal pastimes of his fellow nine-year-olds, Tim had one particular interest that set him apart. Tim collected anything and everything to do with Spider-Man. So when he shut off the light in his room and prepared for an uneventful night of sleep, he was more excited than most would be when a certain wall-crawler decided to pay him a visit (**1**).

Spider-Man had first heard about Timothy from an article in the *Daily Bugle* by columnist Jacob Conover. Timothy had scrapbooks overflowing with newspaper and magazine articles about his idol, and even video footage from Spider-Man's early TV appearances. The newspaper profile on Timothy inspired Spidey to take a rare respite from crime fighting and meet his number one fan face to face. But what Spider-Man hadn't taken into consideration was that Timothy was a New Yorker, and prone to being a bit skeptical. When Spidey lifted the boy and his bed above his head with hardly an effort, Tim soon realized that he was actually in the presence of his favorite hero.

Ecstatic about meeting his idol, Tim showed off his scrapbook collection to his visitor (**2**). They flipped through newspaper articles dating back to the beginning of Spider-Man's career, and discussed exactly how Spider-Man got his powers. Spidey even gave his biggest fan a tutorial on how his web-shooters worked (**3**).

But Tim was a curious boy and wasn't about to pass up this once-in-a-lifetime opportunity. He asked Spider-Man exactly why he gave up his life of fame and fortune and began fighting crime in the first place. And surprisingly, Spider-Man was honest with the young man. He told him about the Burglar he'd failed to stop, and about how that man went on to murder someone who was very close to him. Somehow Timothy understood, and couldn't begrudge his hero for the mistakes of his past (**4**).

The conversation grew lighter then, as the two continued their trip down memory lane. Tim showed Spider-Man bullets he had dug out of a wall of a bank on one occasion after some attempted robbers fired at Spidey and missed. The two even shared a good laugh at a scrapbook Tim kept of retractions that J. Jonah Jameson had been forced to print in the *Daily Bugle* after he had been proven wrong on his assumptions about the wall-crawler (**5**).

Soon Spider-Man realized how late it was getting, so he tucked the boy in, and walked away toward the window to make his exit (**6**). But just as Spider-Man was about to leave, Tim called out one last favor of the hero. He asked Spider-Man if he would take off his mask and show him his true face. And to his surprise, Spider-Man did just that (**7**).

Spider-Man told the boy that his name was Peter Parker, that he was a photographer for the *Daily Bugle*, and that he had shot most of the photos in the articles they had just flipped through. Amazed by the trust his hero placed in him, young Tim swore himself to secrecy, and gave Spider-Man—Peter Parker—a hug before he left (**8**). Spider-Man cast a few weblines, and then departed out of the boy's window (**9**). A second later, Spider-Man paused on a nearby wall and took a moment to collect himself (**10**). And then he swung into the night away from the Slocum-Brewer Cancer Clinic (**11**).

Because Tim Harrison was different from most boys his age. Tim Harrison had been diagnosed with leukemia, and only had a few more weeks to live.

> ### "It's our secret! Forever and ever... I promise."
> **Timothy Harrison**

OUT WITH THE OLD

One minute, Spider-Man was on Earth, investigating a strange edifice in Central Park. The next, he was summoned to a faraway galaxy by a near-omnipotent being called the Beyonder. The Beyonder forced Spidey and a host of other heroes and villains into combat on a planet called Battleworld, and in the course of the many fights, Spider-Man's costume was left in tatters.

The alien costume spread over Peter Parker's form, reacting to his thoughts.

Spider-Man found a machine on Battleworld that seemingly replaced his old uniform with a new black alien version.

THE SAGA OF THE ALIEN COSTUME

When Spider-Man returned from an epic battle of Super Hero versus Super Villain on a far away planet known as Battleworld, he brought with him a souvenir of sorts: a sleek new black costume that would forever change his life.

Spidey's new costume was able to generate a seemingly endless supply of webbing and could change its appearance at will, even mimicking Peter's street clothes.

IN WITH THE NEW

After defeating the villains and escaping the Beyonder, the heroes returned to Earth, and Spider-Man took his alien costume with him. Adopting it as his new uniform, Peter and his alien costume were always in some kind of psychic contact, even when physically separated. If the costume was in a different room, it came at Peter's mental summons.

NIGHT TERRORS

Each night while Peter slept, the alien costume secretly slipped over him and took the unconscious Spider-Man wall-crawling at night, craving the adrenaline that Peter's body produced. The web-swinger awoke each morning with no memory of his nocturnal adventures but utterly exhausted. He suspected something was off, but couldn't suspect the amazing truth.

Spider-Man's new costume could fire webbing from the back of his wrists, a fact the Puma discovered firsthand, much to his own regret.

IT'S ALIVE!

Feeling tired and drained, Spider-Man went to Reed Richards, alias Mr. Fantastic of the Fantastic Four, for help. After a series of tests, Mr. Fantastic made a startling pronouncement. Instead of a suit composed of an unknown extraterrestrial fabric, Spidey's new costume was a living creature. It was a sentient symbiote that had formed a mental and physical bond with the web-swinger.

A MIND OF ITS OWN

As soon as the symbiote's secret was revealed, it attempted to permanently graft itself to Spider-Man's body. Spider-Man did all he could to escape from the costume, but the symbiote tightened its grip on him, almost crushing Spidey in the process. Luckily, Reed Richards had discovered that the symbiote was vulnerable to certain sound frequencies. Using these sound waves, Richards managed to separate Spidey from the costume. At last our hero was free and the alien was imprisoned.

THE BELL TOLLS

Later, the symbiote escaped from the laboratory and pounced on the unsuspecting Spider-Man. In utter desperation, Spider-Man lured the alien to the bell tower of Our Lady Of Saints Church. He knew that the sound of the bells could free him from the symbiote. The alien, knowing that only one of them could survive the ordeal, sacrificed itself to save Peter.

There was a time when the world marveled at his physical prowess. A period when his courage inspired awe and his exploits drew envy. But that was before he met Spider-Man and knew failure and humiliation. It was time for Kraven the Hunter to regain his glory for one last hunt.

KRAVEN'S LAST HUNT

BURIED ALIVE

Kraven was still faster than a panther and stronger than a great ape, but he knew that he was no longer in his prime. He believed that he would never know peace unless he humbled Spider-Man. Formulating a daring plan, a deranged Kraven immersed himself in Spider-Man's essence by burying his body within a veritable mountain of spiders and by using jungle herbs and potions to expand his consciousness and prepare himself mentally. And then he took the fight straight to the spider.

Spider-Man was out web-swinging one night when he was suddenly attacked, drugged, and captured by Kraven. As the hunter advanced on his prey, Spider-Man was unconcerned. Until, that is, he saw the rifle and the look in Kraven's eyes. Aiming the rifle at Spider-Man, Kraven shot the wall-crawler in the head. After which, the villain took the wall-crawler's body back to his estate, placed him in a coffin, and buried him in the grounds.

Although Kraven had defeated his enemy, he didn't feel satiated. He still felt the need to prove his superiority.

But despite finally besting his longtime foe, Kraven wasn't satisfied. In his mind, he had to *become* his enemy to prove his superiority. So, Kraven dressed in Spider-Man's costume, and began to patrol the city, dispensing his own vicious brand of justice, killing some of the criminals he came across.

Posing as Spider-Man, Kraven even rescued Mary Jane from muggers, but she immediately saw through his disguise.

VERMIN

A malicious face from Spider-Man's past, the incredibly strong and animalistic Vermin stalked the Manhattan streets during Kraven's tenure as Spider-Man. Kraven used his skills to track the monster through the sewers, and captured the villain.

RESURRECTION

As Kraven claimed victory over Vermin, the real Spider-Man stirred—he had only been drugged by Kraven. Buried deep in the ground, Peter opened his eyes. Desperate to be reunited with Mary Jane, he broke his way free of the coffin and clawed his way to the surface. Two weeks had passed since Kraven had buried him alive.

THE CHALLENGE

After clawing his way out of the ground and reuniting with Mary Jane, Spider-Man tracked down Kraven. Filled with fury, the wall-crawler attacked the hunter, who didn't bother to resist. Kraven merely smiled. From his skewed perspective, he had won. He had allowed his old enemy to live when he could have easily killed him. Kraven had finally proven himself superior to his arch foe.

Kraven led Spider-Man to a cage where he was keeping Vermin hostage, and attempted to make the web-slinger battle the beast. When Spider-Man refused Kraven's challenge to fight Vermin, the confused monster attacked him anyway. Kraven immediately acted to save Spider-Man, his point already proven in his deranged mind.

Finally feeling satiated, Kraven released Vermin, who could not wait to be free from Kraven's daily torture.

"THEY SAID MY MOTHER WAS INSANE."

THE FINAL KILL

Although Spider-Man was defeated by Vermin, Kraven let his foe leave to pursue the dangerous beast. Kraven finally realized that Spidey was indeed a good man, and felt the hero was no longer his concern. Having proved he could defeat Spider-Man and filled with a sense of peace, Kraven put a shotgun to his own head and committed suicide.

THE WEDDING?

It was the wedding of the century. Peter Parker and Mary Jane Watson finally settled down and promised themselves to each other for the rest of their lives. But sadly, their marriage wasn't built to last. In fact, it never actually happened in the first place.

Peter and Mary Jane were the perfect couple, and their union could even bring a tear to the eye of J. Jonah Jameson.

THE BIG DAY

Peter had wanted to marry his longtime girlfriend Mary Jane for some time. After rejecting Peter's first few marriage proposals due to unresolved family problems, Mary Jane finally realized that it was time to stop running away from things.

Peter originally proposed to Mary Jane by giving her a box of Cracker Jacks. The prize inside was a diamond ring.

ONE MOMENT IN TIME

Peter and Mary Jane had been happily married for many years. Like most married couples, they had gone through countless ups and downs together. But a demon named Mephisto changed all that.

Years after the day Peter and MJ said "I do," Aunt May was shot with a sniper's bullet meant for Spider-Man. While the woman who had been like a mother to him was lying on her deathbed, Peter was visited by the demon Mephisto. He promised Peter a return to health for May, but at a high cost. A demon who thrived on unhappiness, Mephisto wanted to not only end Peter and Mary Jane's relationship, but he wanted to ensure that the couple never got married in the first place. Feeling as if there was no other choice, Peter and Mary Jane agreed to the demon's terms, and everything changed.

In this new reality, Peter never made it to the church on time. His life as Spider-Man caused him to be too late for the event, and it forced Mary Jane to reexamine their relationship. She decided that they could never be married, but didn't want to end everything with Peter. So the couple stayed together, and had all the same adventures as they originally had lived, only they were never husband and wife. But this time, May survived the fatal gunshot, and in the wake of that tragedy, Mary Jane broke up with Peter, worried that her family would be put in danger again because of her relationship with Spider-Man.

Years later, Peter and Mary Jane talked about their break-up, becoming stronger friends once everything was out in the open.

Mary Jane and Peter had been the loves of each other's lives. They understood each other's weaknesses, and relied on each other's strengths.

She accepted Peter's proposal in the less-than-romantic setting of Pittsburgh airport's departure lounge.

However, as the big day approached, Peter began to have doubts. He remembered his former girlfriend Gwen Stacy, and wondered what direction his life might have taken if she hadn't died. Mary Jane also had qualms, and a number of her old boyfriends tried to dissuade her from marrying Peter.

On their wedding day, neither Peter nor Mary Jane arrived on time. Their friends feared that they both had cold feet, but the couple finally showed up, and were married by Mary Jane's uncle, Judge Spencer Watson. They were pronounced Mr. and Mrs. Parker. But that's not how it really happened...

VENOM LEGACY

The Venom symbiote has been passed down to many individuals during its existence. As Scorpion, Mac Gargan was one of Spider-Man's most dangerous foes. But when he adopted Eddie Brock's alien symbiote costume and became Venom, he was nearly unstoppable. And when Peter Parker's school bully Flash Thompson was given a chance to emulate Spidey, a new Venom was born.

The symbiote recruited Mac to be his host, enjoying the criminal's angry mindset.

A DEADLIER VENOM

When Eddie Brock originally donned his living alien costume, he formed a bond with the creature that was so strong, he never imagined he would give up the power and closeness the two shared as Venom. However, after years of wearing the symbiote suit, and discovering that his body was stricken with cancer, Eddie knew his time was almost up. He decided to make amends by parting with the costume. He somehow managed to separate himself from it long enough to sell it at an underground criminal auction.

Soon the suit found its way into the hands of criminal Mac Gargan, and the two beings bonded instantly. Mac abandoned his role as the Scorpion in order to upgrade to a new identity: Venom. Brutal and oftentimes cannibalistic, this new savage Venom eventually found employment with the corrupt Norman Osborn, and even tricked the world into believing he was the true Spider-Man for a time.

The high bidder at Brock's Venom auction was Don Fortunato, who gave the suit to his son Angelo. Venom rejected the weak teen in favor of Mac Gargan.

Just when Spidey thought he'd learned how to handle Eddie Brock's Venom, the alien upgraded to an even more ruthless host.

A FORCE FOR GOOD

Flash Thompson always wanted to be a hero. Growing up around Spider-Man, Flash had even tried to impersonate the wall-crawler when the need arose. As the chairman of Spider-Man's fan club, Flash learned from Spidey's heroic example, and strived to be a better person.

He took the lessons Spidey taught him to war as a soldier, and during one fateful trip, lost his legs in a successful effort to save a fellow troop member. Thinking his life of action was over, Flash was amazed when he was recruited by the military for a clandestine project that would not only see him regain his mobility, but also grant him superhuman abilities. Flash was handpicked to be the new Venom, wearing the living alien suit for covert missions. The military was aware that the symbiote would bond with its host given the opportunity. Consequently, Flash was only allowed to wear the suit for 48 hours at a time.

Flash accepted the challenge of being Venom and in doing so, fulfilled his lifelong dream of becoming a costumed hero. Whether Flash's willpower is strong enough to curb Venom's primal bloodlust is yet to be seen, but Flash intends to do his best to see that Venom stays on the side of good this time around.

The military has installed a kill switch that will destroy the user if he loses control of the symbiote.

Flash is reliant on a wheelchair, but, as Venom, he uses a pair of organic legs—as well as Venom's myriad powers.

Venom has taken a toll on Flash's civilian life. It is always on his mind, and he's been forced to lie to his girlfriend Betty Brant, in order to keep his double identity a secret.

With three titles already under his belt (*The Amazing Spider-Man, The Spectacular Spider-Man,* and *Web of Spider-Man*), the 1990s saw the most popular addition of all, the birth of the adjective-less *Spider-Man*. But while the era started bright, things were about to take a controversial turn.

THE
1990s

If you ask nearly any comic book fan to sum up Spider-Man's adventures in the 1990s with one word, the one answer you're sure to hear more often than not is "clone." While the '90s saw Spidey rise to the height of his popularity, most fans can't get the massive crossover tale dubbed the Clone Saga out of their heads. And that may not be such a bad thing.

With artist sensation Todd McFarlane taking his work from the pages of *The Amazing Spider-Man,* to his own book titled simply *Spider-Man,* Marvel saw the debut issue of the wall-crawler's new adventures sell in the millions. The comic book boom had begun, and Spider-Man was leading the pack. But as the decade progressed, Marvel began to notice the success DC was having with their giant crossovers, and decided to concoct one for Spidey. While the fan base was split on the controversial Clone Saga that followed, the tale proved to stand the test of time, and is still argued about in fan circles today. The Clone Saga once again reinforced just how much Peter Parker means to his reading audience.

SPIDER-MAN #1

"But I've got to tell you, when it comes right down to it, I can be pretty awesome if I want."

PETER PARKER

EDITOR-IN-CHIEF
Tom DeFalco

COVER ARTIST, WRITER, PENCILER, AND INKER
Todd McFarlane

LETTERER
Rick Parker

COLORIST
Bob Sharen

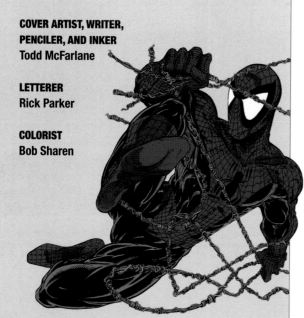

MAIN CHARACTERS: Spider-Man; the Lizard; Mary Jane Watson-Parker; Calypso
MAIN SUPPORTING CHARACTER: Ralph Dill
MAIN LOCATIONS: Various streets of New York City; Calypso's mysterious Upper East Side sanctuary; Peter Parker's SoHo apartment

BACKGROUND

During the biggest comic book boom in the 1990s, you didn't get any bigger than Todd McFarlane. An artist who seemingly crept out of nowhere on titles like DC's *Infinity Inc.* and Marvel's *Incredible Hulk*, Todd McFarlane exploded onto the scene with *The Amazing Spider-Man* alongside writer David Michelinie. Todd's drawing style was noticeably dynamic, adding flair and energy to everything from Spider-Man's exaggerated swinging positions to the weblines he shot from his wrists. Suddenly, Spider-Man was flashy, exciting, and the hero to watch.

So it only made sense for Marvel's editorial team to give Todd McFarlane all the room he wanted to play. The result was *Spider-Man #1*, the first issue in a brand new ongoing series launched in 1990, which showcased McFarlane's talents. Not only was he the penciler and inker of the fledgling title, but he was also named the writer as well. And as expected, the readers devoured the issue, causing it to sell a record-breaking two million copies, and to shoot to the top of every comic store's most demanded issue list.

While McFarlane would soon leave Marvel to found his own comic company, Image Comics, with a few fellow luminaries, Marvel was left with a popular mainstay title that lasted 98 issues before it came to its end in 1998.

THE STORY

While Spider-Man busies himself in his home life with Mary Jane and with stopping an average mugger, a sinister force is building beneath his beloved city.

There was something growing in the corners of New York City. Something evil was lurking just beyond the view of the thousands of citizens going about their daily lives. A veritable force of nature was preparing her bid for revenge—and now all the pieces were falling into place. But above the crowded streets, away from the growing tension, Spider-Man swung through the air on a thin webline, blissfully ignorant of what was brewing somewhere else in the dark.

Soon night arrived, and with it, came the things only found in the shadows. A woman frightened out of her mind, a man desperate for the contents of her purse, and a gun just inches from her face (**1**). They were the sorts of things Spider-Man was used to. Everyday horrors birthed in Manhattan's crevices. But as he dropped onto the scene, surrounded by his own makeshift web, it seemed Spider-Man himself might be the most terrifying thing that the night had to offer (**2**). The rescue was routine for the web-crawler. He saved the woman, captured the man, and shattered the gun. But what was happening across town was anything but commonplace. A woman named Calypso was concocting a potion (**3**), causing a ferocious creature called the Lizard to rise from the depths of the sewers (**4**).

Back in the safety of his SoHo apartment, relaxing in the arms of his wife Mary Jane, Spider-Man had shed his costume and returned to life as normal New York citizen, Peter Parker (**5**). But outside, in the humid air of the city, a primal sound was reverberating. Under its influence, the Lizard was feeding—first on a rat, and then on the human equivalent: criminals and thieves (**6**). Although mostly acting on animal instinct and at the will of the unseen Calypso, the human trapped inside the Lizard took the time to label his kill. In blood, on the wall behind his victims, he wrote the letters "CNNR", standing for Connors (**7**)—his human name. A name far removed from the raving beast he'd become. For Spider-Man, it would be the first clue to a murder mystery that would test his resolve, his endurance, and even his humanity.

As Spider-Man swung happily from rooftop to rooftop (**8**), he was oblivious to the creature that lurked below. Darkness loomed and the Lizard hid in the shadows. Dinner came in the form of poor Ralph Dill, who took an ill-fated shortcut to work (**9**). And the Lizard waited. His plan? To crush Spider-Man (**10**).

As the story continued in the following four issues, Spider-Man and the Lizard clashed in a bloody battle, as savage as any either had ever faced. Eventually, the trail of pain led to Calypso, the former ex-lover of Kraven the Hunter, and a master of the darkest voodoo arts. Having surrendered herself to the forces of evil years earlier, Calypso wanted nothing more than another soul to claim for her own. Spider-Man would go on to defeat the voodoo witch and her unwitting reptilian pet. However, when the smoke cleared, Peter Parker did not feel the return to normalcy that usually accompanied a job well done.

There was something still out there. And it was bad. And it was dark.

"It crawls below. Waiting. Hungering for a hero that swings above it all. Soon it will feast."

May 1993

GIANT-SIZED 200th ISSUE

MARVEL COMICS

$2.95 US
$3.75 CAN
200 MAY

THE SPECTACULAR SPIDER-MAN

THE SPECTACULAR SPIDER-MAN

#200

*"Let's **face** it... people like you and me... we're better off **dead**."*

THE GREEN GOBLIN (HARRY OSBORN)

EDITOR-IN-CHIEF
Tom DeFalco

COVER ARTIST
Sal Buscema

WRITER
J.M. DeMatteis

PENCILER
Sal Buscema

INKER
Sal Buscema

COLORIST
Bob Sharen

LETTERER
Joe Rosen

MAIN CHARACTERS: Spider-Man; the Green Goblin (Harry Osborn); Mary Jane Watson-Parker; Liz Osborn
MAIN SUPPORTING CHARACTERS: Norman Osborn Jr.; J. Jonah Jameson
MAIN LOCATIONS: Harry Osborn's apartment; The Brooklyn Bridge; Peter Parker's apartment; the *Daily Bugle* office; Tony's Italian Kitchen; The Osborn Foundation building

BACKGROUND

Anniversary issues are a longtime tradition in the comic book world. Fans have grown accustomed to finding the payoffs to big stories in an issue #50 or #100 of their favorite titles.

The Spectacular Spider-Man #200 focused on the climax to Harry Osborn's long-running story. Lapsing in and out of drug-induced bouts of insanity since the death of his father, Norman Osborn (the original Green Goblin), Harry's mental illness took center stage in this issue, in what was intended to be the final chapter in his life. And while the 2008 Brand New Day storyline would bring Harry back from the supposed dead, writer J.M. DeMatteis's powerful tale alongside Sal Buscema's unflinching imagery capitalized on the use of silent comic panels to add to the impact of the story they were concocting. The overall effect was an issue truly worthy of the benchmark #200 that graced its cover.

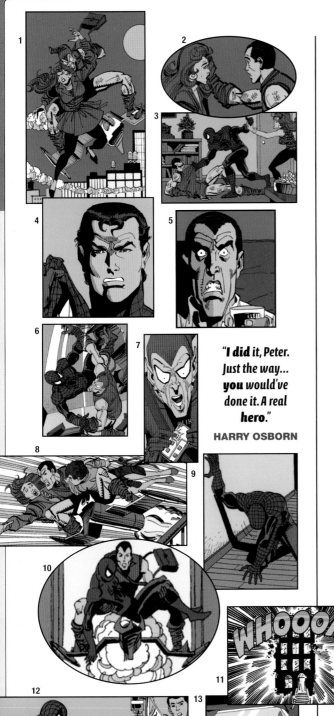

"I did it, Peter. Just the way... you would've done it. A real hero."

HARRY OSBORN

THE STORY

Harry Osborn finally loses his battle with sanity and relapses into the Green Goblin for one seemingly final face off with Spider-Man.

It all started when Harry Osborn witnessed the death of his father. In what would be a traumatic event for any person to go through, the scene that played out in front of Harry Osborn's eyes was much more bizarre and twisted than anything he should have been forced to witness. Because Harry Osborn's father was Norman Osborn, the original Green Goblin. And the person Harry blamed for his death was his best friend, Peter Parker, the amazing Spider-Man.

Since that day, Harry had been in and out of his mind, his insanity growing stronger and stronger over time. Finally, he seemingly gave in to the Goblin inside him, and did what his father before him had done: kidnapped the love of Spider-Man's life, and brought her to the top of the Brooklyn Bridge.

This time it was Spider-Man's wife, Mary Jane Watson-Parker, who found herself the kidnapped victim of the Goblin (**1**). But instead of hurling the woman off the bridge, as his father had done to Gwen Stacy years before, this Green Goblin removed his mask to reveal that Harry Osborn wasn't as far gone as Mary Jane had believed (**2**). True, he blamed Spider-Man for the atrocities committed by his own father, but he had taken Mary Jane there just to let her know that no matter what happened between the Goblin and Spider-Man, he would make sure that she was safe.

Norman then returned Mary Jane to her SoHo loft, a gesture that Spider-Man wasn't pleased with. When the hero returned home after searching the city for any sign of MJ and discovered the Green Goblin there waiting for him, his first reaction was to lash out in anger at Harry (**3**). Mary Jane stopped her husband from his misguided attempt at protecting her, letting Peter know that Harry wasn't there for a fight. After pulling Spider-Man's mask off to look his old friend directly in the eye (**4**), Harry again reassured Mary Jane that she had nothing to fear from him, although he didn't say the same for Peter. Without another word, the Green Goblin flew off into the night, and returned to his own apartment and to Harry Osborn's seemingly normal life with his wife, Liz, and their son, Normie. But even as Harry prepared to open the charitable Osborn Foundation, he plotted the death of Peter Parker (**5**).

Days later, the Green Goblin would finally have the confrontation he was hoping for. Meeting Spider-Man on the rooftop of his Foundation, the two fought it out (**6**), until the Goblin drugged the wall-crawler and then activated a remote timer that would cause the building to explode in the next two minutes (**7**). Not only would Spider-Man die, but the Green Goblin would die with him. But then the unexpected happened, and Harry Osborn's personality once more emerged inside of the Green Goblin. He realized that Mary Jane and his son, Norman Jr., were still in the building that was rigged to blow. So he jumped onto his glider and took Mary Jane and Normie in his arms, flying them to safety (**8**). But the sedated Spider-Man was still on the rooftop (**9**). Until, once again, the Green Goblin surprised everyone by racing back into the building and saving his best friend (**10**). As the Foundation building exploded into a mess of smoke and fire (**11**), the Green Goblin had indeed saved the life of Spider-Man.

Outside on the street, Harry Osborn collapsed. The experimental Goblin formula he had injected himself with was too much for the young man. So like his father before him, Harry seemingly died (**12**), clad in his Green Goblin uniform and with his son present to bare witness. And just like that, Harry became yet another lost life that would weigh on the already burdened conscience of Spider-Man (**13**).

SLASH

"TOO LATE, CARNAGE!"

SPIDER-MAN

"HAPPY HOUR IS OVER!"

MAXIMUM CARNAGE

Spider-Man's world had just gotten a little darker. With the recent apparent death of his former best friend Harry Osborn, Peter thought the worst was behind him. But upstate at the Ravencroft Maximum Security Institution, the serial killer Cletus Kasady was about to prove the wall-crawler dead wrong. Changing into his Carnage alter ego, Kasady escaped the institution for the criminally insane, but not before freeing his fellow inmate—the emotion-altering Shriek. Soon joined by the monstrous, other-worldly Spider-Man Doppelganger, the trio set out at first to hunt down Spider-Man and Venom, and then simply to instigate chaos throughout the city of Manhattan. As his campaign of terror continued, Carnage recruited other powerful allies to his cause of murder and mayhem, including Demogoblin and Carrion. Meanwhile, Spider-Man found himself aided by Black Cat, Cloak, Dagger, Firestar, and even unlikely partners like Morbius and Venom. As the body count of innocent bystanders increased, other heroes like Deathlok, Iron Fist, Captain America, and Nightwatch joined the fray, until a battling Carnage and Venom were caught in a climactic explosion that rendered Carnage unconscious.

Carnage's murder spree caught Spidey off guard because his acts of violence were often random and unpredictable.

THE CLONE SAGA

It was one of the greatest tests of Spider-Man's life. The so-called Clone Saga forced Peter Parker to examine the value of his very existence, and question everything in his life that he had come to know.

ATTACK OF THE CLONE

Five years ago, the Super Villain known as the Jackal had accomplished the unimaginable and cloned Peter Parker. Peter had long thought his perfect duplicate had been destroyed in an explosion that supposedly claimed the life of the Jackal as well. But when both figures from Spider-Man's past reappeared in his world, Spidey was left with more questions than answers. The chief question was this: was Peter the original or merely the clone?

"WALL-CRAWLING IS MY SHTICK... AND THE SPIDER—IS NOTORIOUSLY TERRITORIAL!"
SPIDER-MAN

CARBON COPY

When Peter's Aunt May fell into a coma and her life seemed to be close to its end, Peter's clone returned to New York City to visit her where he encountered the real Spider-Man. Possessing all the original memories and feelings of Peter Parker, the clone felt a strong bond with May and couldn't live with himself if he never spoke to her again.

Now going by the name Ben Reilly, the clone shared Peter's sense of responsibility. So while he knew Peter possessed the right to call himself Spider-Man, Ben decided to adopt a similar costumed appearance and became the hero dubbed the Scarlet Spider by the press.

DYNAMIC DUO

While it took Peter some time to get used to Ben's presence in his life, the two soon became quite the team, and grew to think of each other as a brother. This bond proved very helpful when the Jackal reemerged in their lives and began to play with their minds.

GAMES OF THE JACKAL

Professor Warren aka the Jackal was sure that he could repopulate the world with clones, and had created dozens of Peter Parker doppelgängers to achieve his goal. While Ben and Peter managed to defeat the villain, it wasn't long before the Jackal managed to convince them that Peter was the clone and Ben was the original Spider-Man.

After hearing this revelation, Peter retired and Ben adopted the role of Spider-Man. Shockingly, Norman Osborn was revealed to be the mastermind behind the Clone Saga. Peter was revealed to be the true Spidey when Ben was killed and dissolved to ash.

KAINE

To the world at large, he is a cold-blooded killer, a remorseless assassin-for-hire who leaves his distinctive brand on the faces of his victims. But few know the truth about Kaine. He is actually a clone of Peter Parker, the first of Professor Warren's recreations to reach maturity. However, since Professor Warren was still perfecting his cloning technique, Kaine soon developed a condition called clone degeneration, the symptoms of which have left him horribly scarred.

Kaine believed that Ben Reilly was the original Parker and stalked him across America. He hated Ben, and did all he could to spoil the quality of his life. Kaine thought Peter was a clone like himself, and wanted to protect the life Peter had carved out for himself. With an ever-shifting moral code, Kaine still lurks in the shadows of Spidey's life, walking the line between hero and villain.

April 1995

MARVEL COMICS

400 APR

THE AMAZING SPIDER-MAN 400

"A DEATH IN THE FAMILY..."

DIRECT EDITION

$2.95 US

THE AMAZING SPIDER-MAN #400

"No doctors. No hospitals... This time is for us—to say our good-byes."

AUNT MAY PARKER

EDITOR-IN-CHIEF
Bob Budiansky

COVER ARTISTS
Mark Bagley and Larry Mahlstedt

WRITER
J.M. DeMatteis

PENCILER
Mark Bagley

INKER
Larry Mahlstedt with Randy Emberlin

COLORIST
Bob Sharen

LETTERER
Bill Oakley and NJQ

MAIN CHARACTERS: Spider-Man; Aunt May Parker; the Scarlet Spider; Mary Jane Watson-Parker
MAIN SUPPORTING CHARACTERS: Dr. Julia Caputo; Anna Watson; J. Jonah Jameson; Marla Jameson; Liz Osborn; Norman Osborn Jr.; Flash Thompson; Black Cat; Joe Robertson; Detective Connor Trevane; Lieutenant Jacob Raven
MAIN LOCATIONS: A hospital, New York; Ravencroft Institute; the Parker residence; the Empire State Building; undisclosed cemetery, New York

BACKGROUND

Easily the most controversial storyline ever to shake up the so-called "Spiderverse," the Clone Saga, which was launched in *Web of Spider-Man* #117 (October 1994), had already turned the life of Peter Parker on its ear. It started as just another idea thrown out by writer Terry Kavanagh at a brainstorming summit about bringing back Spider-Man's clone. But when faced with the story potential that could spring out of that simple concept, the idea blossomed into an ambitious comic book event that strived to be something more than the means to nab increased sales.

 The folks in the Spider-Man offices wanted a story with weight and long-lasting consequence. And while her death might not have lasted as long as originally intended, May Parker's final moments in *The Amazing Spider-Man* #400 were meant to be just the kind of weighty story the team set out to tell. Even though it is often hard for good characters to stay dead in the world of comic books, Aunt May's death can still be read as the end of an era it originally signified.

> "Let go. Fly. 'Second to the right—and straight on till morning.'"
>
> **PETER PARKER**

THE STORY

In "The Gift" story, Peter Parker spends his last treasured moments with Aunt May before she seemingly dies, while his clone watches on, unable to say goodbye.

It must have felt like a dream for Spider-Man. His Aunt May had been in a coma for days, and the doctors feared she might never wake up. So when Peter got a call from the hospital, he naturally assumed the worst (**1**). Swinging across town at a breakneck speed, the wall-crawler switched into his civilian identity with a heavy heart and entered the room of the woman who had been like a mother to him. A woman he wasn't ready to say goodbye to.

And luckily for Peter, he wouldn't have to. Because the woman who waited behind the door was as full of life as she'd ever been (**2**). She'd awoken from her coma, and would soon be ready to head home and resume her life. While Peter cried happy tears, he saw something else out of the corner of his eye. Ben Reilly, the Scarlet Spider, was watching the scene from outside (**3**). Although Spider-Man's clone might have been an outcast from the life he'd once thought was his, he couldn't help the fact that he loved Aunt May as if she was his aunt.

May returned to her familiar Forest Hills home to the delightful news that Peter and Mary Jane were expecting a baby (**4**). But just as Peter should have been enjoying this happy family time, the Scarlet Spider appeared from the shadows, intent on having a word with him. As the two talked, the Scarlet Spider revealed his plan. Now that he knew May was going to be OK, the Spider was going to leave the lives of the Parkers forever (**5**).

For a while, life at the Parker residence returned to normal. There was a lot of happy reminiscing about the past, and Aunt May and Peter even took a trip to the top of the Empire State Building to spend a little alone time together. It was there that May revealed to Peter that she'd known about his secret for years (**6**). She'd known he was Spider-Man and although his other life frightened her, she was proud of him just the same. The revelation was a weight off Peter's shoulders, even though it seemed to exhaust the elderly May. The two decided to head home, a new understanding now existing between them in the space where an unmentionable secret used to live.

What Peter didn't know at the time was that May had done what she set out to do. Now her fever had returned, but she wasn't fighting any longer (**7**). It was her time, and she knew it. Even though Peter still wasn't ready, May was. So he held her hand, and talked to her softly about a book she'd read to him as a child. May fell asleep and Peter and Mary Jane mourned her passing (**8**).

Outside May's window, another man was feeling her loss. A man who had sworn to leave the Parkers alone. A man dressed in a red and blue spider costume who was affected by Aunt May's death just as deeply as any of those lucky enough to be standing by her side (**9**).

It was cold on the day they buried May Parker. Peter and Mary Jane stood among a crowd of some of their closest friends and tried to keep their emotions in check (**10**). May's casket was lowered into the ground, and soon enough, the crowd dispersed and people went back to their daily lives. Peter and MJ were the last to leave. No words were spoken. Only an unsaid understanding passed between the two before they too left the cemetery.

And then another silent mourner arrived. Ben Reilly wasn't able to say goodbye to his "aunt," but still needed to pay his respects to the woman who had so influenced his life. Placing a single rose on the fresh earth before her tombstone, Reilly let himself cry, mourning not just May, but the life that he had never truly known (**11**).

IDENTITY CRISIS

"...THIS NEW IDENTITY IS GIVING US A CLEAN START, GIVING US OUR LIVES BACK!"

SPIDER-MAN AS THE HORNET

After his resurrection, Norman Osborn proved that he wasn't the Green Goblin and cleared his own name. He also succeeded in framing Spidey, placing a $5 million reward on the hero's head. With every bounty hunter gunning for him, Peter Parker needed a new secret identity...

MULTIPLE PERSONALITY

Peter knew that other costumed heroes had temporarily adopted new identities in the past, but he also knew that they were always exposed. He wanted to beat the odds and decided to adopt more than one new alter ego. Realizing that it would be difficult to juggle different personas at the same time, he decided that each one would reflect some aspect of his real personality or powers.

RICOCHET

While searching through the used clothing section at a local thrift shop, Mary Jane discovered a leather jacket with a distinctive letter "R" on its back. Using that insignia as her starting point, she designed another new costume for her husband. Peter used his spiderlike agility to pretend that he was a super-athlete called Ricochet.

Ricochet was a wisecracking hero, annoyingly often in the middle of a battle.

Richochet seemed to be a less than law-abiding member of society.

Spider-Man wouldn't have been able to conceive of his new identities without Mary Jane's enthusiastic help.

DUSK

Spider-Man had visited an alternate dimension a few weeks earlier called the Negative Zone and had acquired a costume that allowed him to merge with shadows and become practically invisible. Peter decided to call this dark persona Dusk. The mysterious Dusk employed a utility belt that contained gas, smoke, and stun grenades.

As Dusk, Spider-Man spied on the underworld by pretending to be a criminal mercenary.

Dusk's ability to blend into shadows made him a monstrous creature of the night.

As Prodigy, Peter advocated strong morals.

PRODIGY

Conceived and designed entirely by Mary Jane, Prodigy was the consummate costumed hero. He possessed superhuman strength, a bulletproof costume, and could leap from one rooftop to the next with a single bound.

Protecting people from villains like Roughhouse, Prodigy was like the comic-book archetypes of Peter's youth. Prodigy became a media darling, achieving the fame and respect that had eluded Spidey.

Not realizing who was wearing the costume, the Human Torch confronted the Hornet after hearing the "new" hero make a public statement about how Spidey was no longer a problem.

Though the jetpack was far too heavy for a normal man to carry, Spider-Man had no trouble with it.

HORNET

Peter went to visit his old friend Hobie Brown, an electronics wizard and inventor who was also the Prowler. Hobie had recently invented a cybernetically controlled jetpack and he gifted it to Spider-Man for his new Hornet identity.

The Hornet could fly at nearly 50 mph (80 kph).

SLINGERS

A few months after Peter was able to prove Spider-Man's innocence and retire his four new identities, someone else reactivated them. Dan Lyons was an old man who had once been a costumed crime-fighter known as the Black Marvel. He gathered four young misfits and gave them Spidey's faux identities and powers, forming a new team of heroes called the Slingers.

"HANDS OFF THE GEEK, SCORPION! YOU AND I HAVE SOME UNFINISHED BUSINESS TO TAKE CARE OF!"

SPIDER-MAN IMPOSTER

When Peter crossed paths with the Scorpion, he discovered the villain had a new look, complete with a power upgrade.

EARLY RETIREMENT

Peter Parker was through with being Spider-Man. But unfortunately, Spider-Man wasn't quite finished with Peter Parker. After his latest battle with the Green Goblin, Spidey had hung up his webs to concentrate on his real life. But while at a job interview at the Tri Corp Research Foundation, not only did Peter run into the Super Villain Scorpion, but he also encountered a new Spider-Man.

A NEW CHAPTER

Spider-Man's life had been a chaotic mess of late. He'd been led through a maze of misdirection, where death and resurrection seemed to haunt him at every turn. It was time to finally get his life back on track. It was time to embark on a new chapter.

MAY'S RETURN

The reports of Aunt May's death were greatly exaggerated. As part of his master plan to toy with Peter Parker's life, Norman Osborn had hired an actress to portray May, while he had kidnapped the original. Peter had watched the actress die, not his beloved aunt, and he was now thrilled to have her back in his life.

CALL OF DUTY

Though retirement seemed to agree with Peter, he eventually resumed his responsibilities and returned to the role that he was born to play. Spider-Man went back into action and fought new villains such as the Ranger, Shadrac, and Captain Power.

During Spider-Man's retirement, a new Spider-Man appeared on the scene. Peter had no idea who this super-powered individual was, but when the imitator was bested by the villain Shadrac, Peter came to the novice's rescue, and realized that the new Spider-Man was in fact a teenage girl.

Peter returned to protecting the innocent from thugs, criminals, and Super Villains.

Spider-Man will always be haunted by his noble sense of responsibility.

After Peter reclaimed his Spider-Man mantle to battle Shadrac, his replacement decided to adopt her own Super Hero identity and became the new Spider-Woman. Revealed to secretly be teenager Mattie Franklin, she soon became a hero in her own right.

MOVING ON UP

While he still visited the old homestead once in a while, Peter Parker and Mary Jane had moved in to a deluxe condo in Manhattan, using the money Mary Jane earned in her modeling career. Aunt May even moved in with the young couple at their spacious penthouse duplex.

In November of 1998, *The Amazing Spider-Man* ended, but in January of 1999, *The Amazing Spider-Man* began anew. Entering the new decade with a rebooted franchise and a focus on coherent story before all else, Spider-Man was reshaped for a new millennium of fans.

THE
2000s

In an attempt to distance itself from some of its past continuity, *The Amazing Spider-Man* was relaunched with a new first issue just before the close of the 1990s. But it wasn't until 2001 and the title's 30th issue that the new direction of the web-slinger became apparent to the fans. Writer J. Michael Straczynski took ahold of Peter Parker's life and, with the guidance of new Editor-in-Chief Joe Quesada, helped chart a bold new direction for the character that relied on crafting five- or six-issue story arcs that could be repackaged in trade paperbacks for the book store market. Sales skyrocketed, and with help from writer Brian Michael Bendis's re-imagined teenaged version of Peter Parker in the blockbuster hit *Ultimate Spider-Man*, Spidey was once again the character to watch.

The numbering would soon return to that of the original series, and Spider-Man would once again be treated to a soft reboot in 2008's Brand New Day storyline. With the help of a few incredibly popular blockbuster movies, Spider-Man remains Marvel's favorite son.

EZEKIEL

An eccentric, mysterious millionaire with abilities alarmingly like Spider-Man's, Ezekiel appeared suddenly in Peter Parker's life and turned it upside down. Spewing tales of totems and animal-powered warriors, Ezekiel put a whole new spin on the life Peter thought he knew.

Ezekiel had a special adamantium-encased room built for Spider-Man to allow the wall-crawler to hide in safety from Morlun for months if necessary. However, Peter turned down Ezekiel's offer, preferring to face his opponent head-on.

ORIGIN

The bulk of Ezekiel's personal history is a mystery. The only things known about the enigmatic man's past are secrets that he himself has divulged, and they may have been altered to better achieve his personal goals.

When he first appeared in Spider-Man's life, he told Peter that his spider-powers were not merely the by-product of a scientific accident. According to Ezekiel, Peter Parker was the newest appointee in a long line of animal-powered warriors. He then warned Peter of the predator Morlun, who would feed on those totemistic abilities. When Spider-Man and Ezekiel eventually fought Morlun, these far-fetched theories suddenly seemed much more legitimate.

As Ezekiel continued to appear in Spider-Man's life at moments of crisis, the pair struck up a friendship of sorts. But lurking behind Ezekiel's benevolent façade was his true motivation. During an ancient bloodletting ritual, Ezekiel had gained spider-powers that were very similar to Peter's. But Ezekiel was told that there could only be one true spider warrior, and he intended to sacrifice Peter so that he alone could survive.

Ezekiel obtained his spider-powers through a bloodletting ritual in South America. He was warned that he would have to eliminate the true spider warrior—or be eliminated himself.

After luring Spider-Man back to South America, Ezekiel managed to best the hero. There he summoned a spider god-like entity and tricked it into thinking that Peter was the fake spider champion and worthy of sacrifice.

Ezekiel possessed Spider-Man's ability to cling to surfaces.

Ezekiel encouraged Peter to trust him—a trust he would later exploit.

KEY DATA

FIRST APPEARANCE: *The Amazing Spider-Man* (2nd series) #30 (June 2001)

FULL NAME: Ezekiel Sims

AFFILIATIONS: None

POWERS/ABILITIES: Ezekiel possessed enhanced strength, speed, reflexes, agility, and resilience that were only slightly less intense than Spider-Man's. He could also adhere to surfaces and possessed an uncanny early warning "spider-sense." Due to their similar powers, Ezekiel could also bypass Spidey's own spider-sense.

Ezekiel and Peter developed a mentor/protégé relationship. Ezekiel helped Peter understand a side to his powers that he never knew existed.

When Ezekiel was forced to offer Peter to the spider god in his place, he couldn't go through with it. He realized the good that Peter had done with his gifts, while he had squandered his own. Ezekiel attacked the spider and sacrificed himself so that the true spider champion would live.

MORLUN

A predator by nature, Morlun existed to feed off people with animal-based powers. To someone with arachnid abilities like Spider-Man, Morlun was as dangerous as they came.

Morlun had been alive for hundreds of years, stalking and feeding on his prey.

Morlun was tougher than he looked. At times, he possessed super-strength that could rival that of the incredible Hulk and Thor.

Morlun could only survive by sucking the energy out of other super-powered beings, particularly those with animal-based powers. But the longer he went without feedings, the weaker he would become.

Even though Dex shot and supposedly killed Morlun, Spider-Man let the servant escape. Spider-Man realized the torment that Morlun had put his former servant through, and knew Dex's action was more of a case of self defense than cold-blooded murder.

ORIGIN

Shortly after his first encounter with Ezekiel, Spider-Man met his opposite number in the energy vampire named Morlun. Although his past was just as cloudy as Spider-Man's new mentor, Ezekiel's, Morlun did not possess animal-based powers, but instead fed on them. A deadly being, Morlun had lived for centuries by absorbing the life-force of super-powered victims. Morlun traveled to New York specifically to prey on Spider-Man. There he began to wreak havoc in order to gain the web-slinger's attention before challenging the hero to physical combat. Spidey soon realized that Morlun's strength was like nothing he had ever faced before, and knew that continuing to challenge Morlun hand-to-hand would be futile. Spider-Man was finally able to lure Morlun to a nuclear power plant, where he weakened his foe with dangerous radiation. After this, Morlun was shot and seemingly killed by his manservant, Dex, who was tired of his master's constant abuse.

Morlun liked to savor his kill, and took the time to be as prepared as possible for his fight with Spider-Man.

Morlun never tired, and was able to track any superhuman after merely making contact with his or her skin.

KEY DATA

FIRST APPEARANCE: *The Amazing Spider-Man* (2nd series) #30 (June 2001)

ALIAS: None

AFFILIATIONS: None

POWERS/ABILITIES: Morlun possessed super strength that he drew directly from beings with animal-based powers. Able to live for centuries given the proper energy sources, Morlun could track his superhuman victims by simply touching them.

THE NEW AVENGERS

Initially composed of Spider-Man, Spider-Woman, Captain America, Iron Man, and Luke Cage, the New Avengers' first official mission took them to the prehistoric Savage Land, where they were joined by Wolverine. The powerhouse Sentry and the enigmatic Ronin soon added to their numbers. From tackling organized crime in Japan to mutant threats in Canada, the New Avengers quickly proved they were just as formidable as their original counterparts.

When Electro caused a breakout at the Raft, New York's maximum security prison, Spider-Man found himself allied with other heroes in order to quell the riots. Convinced their gathering was fate, Captain America took it upon himself to create an all-new team of Super Heroes—the New Avengers.

Spider-Woman
Despite enjoying a lengthy career as a hero, Jessica Drew didn't officially join the Avengers until this recent incarnation. Although raised to be an agent of the villainous Hydra, Jessica has proven herself a hero time and time again.

Spider-Man
Before the New Avengers, Peter had only been granted reserve Avenger status despite his years as a dedicated crime-fighter. So, he couldn't say no to his chance to join the team when personally recruited by Captain America.

The Sentry
Possessing the power of "a million exploding suns," the Sentry served on the New Avengers. At the same time he was constantly combating his inner multiple personality disorder and trying to find some semblance of normal life in his chaotic world.

Luke Cage
The heart of the New Avengers, Luke Cage hides his kind personality beneath his dense skin and tough guy attitude. He proved his romantic side when he married former hero Jessica Jones, after the two had a daughter together.

Wolverine

Wolverine constantly tells anyone who will listen that he's a lone wolf. However, he has been employing his mutant powers and razor-sharp adamantium claws for years as part of the X-Men, before also joining the New Avengers.

Captain America

Injected with a super-soldier serum during the days of World War II and later frozen in ice, Captain America is more than just a man. To the hero community he stands as an icon of everything noble and just about the Avengers.

Iron Man

With an unending bank account and a dedication to the Avengers lasting nearly all his adult life, Iron Man Tony Stark was an obvious recruit to the new team. He was easily persuaded after Captain America pointed out how necessary the Avengers are to the safety of our planet.

Ronin

Upon resurrection from an apparent death, the archer Hawkeye was enlisted to the New Avengers. He was passed the mantle of the mysterious Ronin by Echo, a vigilante from Daredevil's past, becoming the second hero to wear the uniform.

The New Avengers have battled some of the most powerful villains on the planet, including an alliance between the nefarious groups H.A.M.M.E.R, Hydra, A.I.M., and the Hand.

THE LATEST NEW AVENGERS

Although they've triumphed over adversity many times in their relatively short tenure as a team, the members of the New Avengers have not walked an easy road. Forced to go underground when Iron Man sided with the government during the Super Hero Civil War, the team defended a world that would eagerly see them arrested on the spot. After surviving that conflict, along with an invasion of shape-shifting Skrull aliens and a government siege on the otherworldly home of the Norse Gods, the team has finally been restored to its rightful and legal place in the world. With Luke Cage as their leader and Captain America giving them his full support, the latest incarnation of this team now includes longtime Avenger Ms. Marvel, former S.H.I.E.L.D. agent and West Coast Avenger Mockingbird, and even the Fantastic Four's famous blue-eyed Thing. As well as loyally serving on the New Avengers, Spider-Man is a member of the Avengers.

THE OTHER

THE DEATH OF SPIDEY

After a ferocious fight on a busy New York City street, Morlun defeated Spider-Man and was about to absorb his entire life-force. However, the villain was interrupted before he could feed on his prey. He returned later to Spider-Man's hospital bed where the hero rested in critical condition. As Morlun approached him, the spider half of Peter's personality took hold, and suddenly he attacked the villain, killing him and feeding on his energy like a wild animal. Afterward, Peter reverted back to normal and finally passed away in Mary Jane's arms.

Despite Peter giving his all to defeat Morlun, he just wasn't strong enough to overcome Morlun's brute strength.

Things were looking bad for the future of Spider-Man. Learning that he had contracted a terminal illness, Peter was trying to come to grips with his own mortality. He was plagued with disturbing dreams, and his powers continued to weaken. His life took yet another turn for the worse when Morlun, who was believed to be dead, returned to hound the wall-crawler. After making his peace with death and spending time with his family, Spider-Man engaged in a final conflict with Morlun, knowing full well that this might be the last adventure Spider-Man ever had. And unfortunately for the friends and family of Peter Parker, the battle was one that Spider-Man would not walk away from.

After their battle, Morlun left Spider-Man battered and defeated, barely clinging to life with little to no hope of survival.

REBIRTH

When a distraught Mary Jane returned home to Avengers Tower, she was shocked to find Peter's body reduced to a lifeless husk that had split open in two, as if something had hatched from inside it. Meanwhile, trapped in some sort of dream state, Peter had found his way beneath a New York City bridge, and somehow encased himself inside a giant cocoon. As he embraced a spider entity in his dream, giving in to his true self, his cocoon in the real world cracked open. Blood began to drip out into the water below, and like a natural birth, Peter's form emerged. Peter splashed into the water, and then dramatically surfaced, now a new man, reborn without a trace of his former injuries. Peter returned to Avengers Tower, and into the arms of Mary Jane and his Aunt May. As he underwent a barrage of scientific tests by his friends in the Super Hero community, and returned to his work as Spider-Man, Peter soon realized a strange new fact. He had not just been resurrected. When he exited his cocoon, Peter had evolved.

NEW SENSES

"EVOLVE OR DIE."

When he returned to the land of the living, Spider-Man discovered that he was much more in tune with his spider half than ever before. The hair on Spidey's arms was more sensitive, like that of a real spider, which in turn increased his ability to better perceive the world around him. Not only were his natural senses magnified, but he could also adhere objects to his back, a natural extension of his old wall-crawling ability.

STINGERS

After his resurrection, Spider-Man soon discovered his most startling new ability. When faced with danger, poisonous stingers would protrude out of his wrists as if by instinct. However, this new power appears to have gone away in the wake of recent events.

THE IRON SPIDER

When Peter Parker returned from the dead with his original costume in tatters, Tony Stark decided to take it upon himself to create a new uniform for his New Avengers teammate. Using the very same sophisticated nanotechnology that he employed in his own Iron Man suit, Stark developed a new look for Spider-Man to aid him in his war on crime.

QUICK CHANGE

Spider-Man adapted to his new costume quite easily. He could use its abilities to fight criminals in ways he wouldn't have been able to before. The new technology allowed him to keep the costume on in public at all times, as it could be made invisible to the naked eye. Using rapid response thought-control, the nanotechnology also let Spidey switch from his Iron Spider look to his street clothes, as well as to his traditional red and blue costume, and even his black uniform.

NOW YOU SEE HIM...

One of the most practical features of the Stark-created costume was that it could blend in with a variety of backgrounds, rendering Spider-Man invisible to his opponents. Already well-versed in stealth techniques, Spidey used the uniform to take his abilities to a whole new level.

Spidey's new costume included lenses with enhanced visual capabilities, letting him see in the infrared and ultraviolet spectrums. This came in handy when stalking criminals and trying to locate their precise positioning.

"I'VE TAKEN THE OPPORTUNITY TO MAKE SOME SLIGHT... IMPROVEMENTS." TONY STARK

Peter believed Stark's true motive for creating the costume was to win Spidey's favor.

Spidey joined forces with Iron Man in the Super Hero Civil War, putting him at odds with Captain America.

Spidey's new suit contained a limited supply of oxygen, which let him stay underwater for great lengths of time without coming up for air. His mask also contained carbon filters in the mouth area to keep out harmful toxins.

UPGRADES

Spider-Man could glide for short distances by opening his arms and allowing mesh webbing in the Stark suit's armpits to catch the air currents. The headpiece boosted Spidey's hearing by amplifying external sounds and it also served as a fire, police, and emergency scanner. In addition, the suit contained a short-range GPS communication system.

WHERE'S WALDO?

Tony Stark developed three mechanical arms, or waldoes, that could extend from Spider-Man's back using thought control. The waldoes could serve as weapons or as an extra set of arms able to pick up objects or foes. They could even be used like makeshift periscopes in order to peer around corners, sending the images directly to Spidey's eyepieces.

BULLETPROOF

Spidey's new suit contained a thinly woven Kevlar layer that was able to withstand small-caliber bullets. Spider-Man was forced to put his new armor to the ultimate test on one of his first trial outings, when he instinctively put himself in harm's way to save an innocent girl's life. Just as Tony Stark had promised, his new armor deflected the bullet without a problem.

The suit was made of an utlra-thin metal micro-fiber.

Stark created Iron Spider suits for a handful of government agents who became known as the Scarlet Spiders.

Spider-Man gave up his Iron Spider costume after he and Iron Man had a falling out over the events of the Civil War.

CIVIL WAR

It turned brother against brother and friends into enemies. Triggered by the passing of the Super Hero Registration Act, the Super Hero Civil War shook the universe to its core, and created divisions that are still not fully mended to this day. And for Spider-Man, it changed everything.

THE STAMFORD TRAGEDY

When the latest incarnation of the Super Hero team known as the New Warriors engaged in a battle with a group of Super Villains, including the volatile criminal Nitro, their fight accidentally caused an explosion that destroyed a school and cost the lives of hundreds of innocents. Looking for a quick solution, the government rushed the Superhuman Registration Act through congress.

At a highly touted press conference, Spider-Man stood in front of the audience wearing his traditional costume. Then much to the public's shock and awe, he removed his mask, outing his identity to the world.

THE ACT

The Superhuman Registration Act meant that every hero and vigilante would be forced to register his or her identity with the government and placed on its payroll. Iron Man supported the Act, and asked Spider-Man to publicly endorse it. When Spider-Man revealed his secret identity to the world, Peter's friends and former employers, including J. Jonah Jameson, were floored by the news, and Peter Parker instantly became a household name.

THE RESISTANCE

Not everyone supported the Registration Act. Captain America considered it an invasion of privacy and a violation of civil rights. And with the Act's passing, the iconic hero became a fugitive merely by standing up for what he believed in. Hunted by Iron Man and other registered heroes, Captain America went underground, joining forces with other like-minded individuals.

Despite sticking by his mentor's side, Spider-Man began to regret his decision to register and make such a public stance. He and his family were hounded by the paparazzi and Super Villains with grudges. His attempt to protect his loved ones had backfired, and he was beginning to see how important his privacy had been. And after the hero Goliath was killed during a battle with Iron Man's forces, Spider-Man had had enough. He abandoned Iron Man and joined Captain America's rebels.

"I THINK THIS PLAN WILL SPLIT US DOWN THE MIDDLE."

CAPTAIN AMERICA

THE GOOD GUYS?

Iron Man wasn't above recruiting Super Villains to his cause. As a member of Captain America's underground resistance, Spider-Man was forced to confront nefarious criminals like Venom and Lady Deathstrike, Wolverine's murderous enemy. It was clear that Iron Man would stop at nothing to prove his point.

After so much bloody violence, Captain America finally looked around and took note of the devastation this war was causing. Like a true hero, he gave up the fight, and turned himself over to Iron Man's custody.

A NEGATIVE PLACE

The fights began to escalate, as Iron Man and company detained any and all unregistered heroes and villains in an other-dimensional prison complex located in the Negative Zone. Captain America's side invaded the stronghold, and directly confronted the registered heroes in yet another brutal battle.

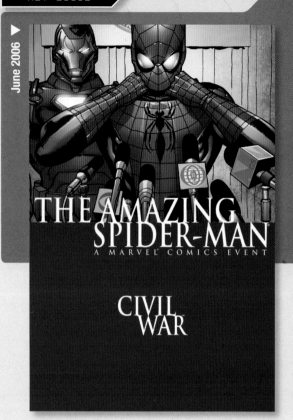

June 2006

THE AMAZING SPIDER-MAN
A MARVEL COMICS EVENT

CIVIL WAR

THE AMAZING SPIDER-MAN #533

"My name is Peter Parker, and I've been Spider-Man since I was fifteen years old."

PETER PARKER

EDITOR-IN-CHIEF
Joe Quesada

COVER ARTIST
Ron Garney

WRITER
J. Michael Straczynski

PENCILER
Ron Garney

INKER
Bill Reinhold

COLORIST
Matt Milla

LETTERER
Cory Petit

MAIN CHARACTERS: Spider-Man; Iron Man; Mary Jane Watson-Parker; Aunt May Parker
MAIN SUPPORTING CHARACTERS: J. Jonah Jameson; Joe Robertson; Mr. Fantastic; Invisible Woman; Pierce McPherson; Flash Thompson; members of Spider-Man's rogues' gallery; various other Super Heroes
MAIN LOCATIONS: Press briefing room, Washington, D.C.; the *Daily Bugle* office; the Baxter Building; Stark Tower; unspecified airfield

BACKGROUND

Writer J. Michael Straczynski had reinvented the Spider-Man franchise at a time when it needed it most. Falling stagnant a few years after John Byrne's revamp, *The Amazing Spider-Man* got a shot in the arm when Straczynski and legendary artist John Romita Jr. started on the title with the 30th issue of the second series. Spider-Man's origins were examined and a mystical layer was added to the mix.

Spidey met the offspring of his greatest enemy and also Gwen Stacy, he gained new powers as a result of The Other storyline, and he earned a new armored costume from Iron Man, Tony Stark. While fans argued about these controversial subjects, the result was just what Marvel had wanted. People were talking about Spider-Man again.

Then came the Civil War. As the greatest heroes split into two factions, Spider-Man had to make a decision that would cause even more controversy.

THE STORY

Spider-Man reveals his secret identity to the world, forcing his friends, family, enemies, and allies to react to the shocking news.

The Super Hero community might have been divided, but Spider-Man had chosen his side. With the looming threat of the Superhuman Registration Act requiring every masked avenger and vigilante to register their powers and identity with the United States government, the heroes couldn't seem to stop arguing among themselves about the constitutionality of this proposed idea. But Peter Parker had to do what was best for his family. And at the time, that meant siding with the law, and his mentor Tony Stark, Iron Man.

Tony had taken Spider-Man under his wing a few months ago, helping the Parker family out when their house was destroyed by a malicious face from Peter's past. So when it came time to pay back Iron Man with his loyalty, Spider-Man stepped up to the plate and did what Tony Stark asked him to do. He went before the public at a highly touted press conference in Washington, D.C., and took off his mask. To show his support for the Registration Act, Peter Parker revealed his secret identity to the world (**1**).

And everything changed. Thirty million people searched the internet simultaneously for the name Peter Parker. In the *Daily Bugle* office, J. Jonah Jameson was shocked (**2**). He threw his coffee mug across his office, betrayed by a young man he'd always thought of as honest and forthright.

Meanwhile, Peter was having conflicted feelings almost rivaling those of the public. Always keeping the safety of Mary Jane and Aunt May in mind, Peter believed in his cause, but not at the cost of his family's wellbeing. So making his way through a mixed hoard of protestors and supporters (**3**), Peter headed to one of Stark's limos to be taken to the airport to return home to New York.

Of course, Peter's greatest supporter was, as always, Mary Jane. Calling her from the limo, Peter talked to MJ before being interrupted by a call on the limo's car phone from Reed Richards of the Fantastic Four (**4**). As Reed, his wife Sue, and even Aunt May chimed in on simultaneous conversations, Peter needed a moment to collect his thoughts, so he webbed the two phones together and continued the rest of the ride to the airport in solitude.

But Spider-Man's homecoming didn't go exactly as he had hoped. First he was greeted by a lawyer who let him know in no uncertain terms that the *Daily Bugle* was suing him for misrepresentation, fraud, and breach of contract (**5**). After that, he had to walk through the densely packed press on the sidewalk surrounding his home at Stark Tower. And the whole time, the world observed via constant TV coverage. Watching from his own home, Flash Thompson assumed the news was some sort of hoax (**6**). While in seedier areas of the city, villains like the Vulture and Dr. Octopus began to plot their revenge (**7**).

But Peter's worst surprise upon returning to New York was Tony Stark's own little twist that he sprung on Peter by way of another press conference. In his public address, Stark announced to the nation that the deadline for registration had come and gone (**8**). Those who chose not to comply would now be hunted down and arrested, with no exceptions. He then went on to announce that he had formed a strike force to combat these underground rebels, and that Spider-Man would be part of it. Shocked, Peter decided to leave the tower for some fresh air, but instead was greeted by another onslaught of the press (**9**), this time complete with an assassination attempt. Peter managed to stop the gunman (**10**), but the Captain America fanatic threatened to sue him for blowing up his hand (**11**). Like it or not, a war between Super Heroes was brewing, and Peter Parker had just been drafted (**12**).

"...so it's best I introduce you to the others you'll be fighting with in this war–before the dying starts tomorrow."

IRON MAN

ONE MORE DAY

It would be the ultimate test of their relationship, and one Mary Jane Watson and Peter Parker would pass with flying colors. Ironically enough, by proving their love for one another, their reward would be to spend the rest of their lives apart. All they had left was one last day together, before a dark force destroyed the relationship that had taken them so long to build.

> " JUST A FEW SECONDS MORE... LISTEN TO ME, PETER, **LISTEN** TO ME. "
> Mary Jane

Peter registered his aunt at the hospital under the name May Morgan to avoid attention.

AUNT MAY

Peter Parker's secret identity became public knowledge in the events leading up to the Super Hero Civil War. Due to the fact that Peter decided to disobey the law and join a group of underground rebels in the fight for Super Hero rights, he had become a fugitive. He was forced to hide his family in a seedy motel in order to avoid attention. But unfortunately, while Iron Man and his forces didn't find Peter's location, the Kingpin did. The crime boss sent an assassin to kill Spider-Man, but the bullet missed its mark and struck Aunt May instead. Clinging to life in a hospital bed, Aunt May's situation looked bleak indeed. The only saving grace was that her bills were paid for by Iron Man Tony Stark. Despite viewing Peter as a fugitive from the law, Tony realized May was an innocent victim, and knew she didn't deserve her fate.

Dr. Strange erased the world's memory of Spidey's alter ego.

> " I WANT YOUR MARRIAGE. "
>
> Mephisto

MEPHISTO

After asking nearly every person he could think of for help to save Aunt May, including Doctor Strange, Spider-Man was out of options. It seemed that no matter what he did, the woman who was like a mother to him was going to die, and it was going to be his fault. But then the devil came to call.

The demon Mephisto was more than a little interested in Peter Parker's situation. He understood the complex destinies of humankind, and knew that even the smallest brushstrokes of a person's life could be altered with dramatic consequences. Mephisto would allow Aunt May a full recovery, but for a price. He wanted to end Peter's relationship with MJ and make it as if their marriage had never happened. Seeing no other choice, Peter and Mary Jane gave in to the demon's terms, after spending one more day together, remembering everything they'd gone through as a couple. As Mephisto changed the world around them, MJ promised Peter that no matter what changed, they would find each other again.

DOCTOR STRANGE

When the doctors first told Peter that there was nothing they could do to help May, he turned to a doctor of a different sort, the master magician Doctor Strange. Although the mage couldn't heal May, he did help Peter visit other heroes and villains all over the planet in a search for aid. Later, Peter visited Dr. Strange again, this time begging the sorcerer to erase the world's knowledge of Spidey's true identity in order to protect his family.

THE NEW STATUS QUO

In the new reality Mephisto concocted, Mary Jane and Peter had never married, but had remained a couple. When May was shot, she recovered, and Spidey had Dr. Strange arrange for the world to forget that he was Spider-Man, with only Mary Jane remembering. Nevertheless the couple broke up when Mary Jane decided she could no longer deal with the dangerous world of Spider-Man.

BRAND NEW DAY

AUNT MAY

Aunt May's health troubles were finally over. Recovering completely from being shot by one of the Kingpin's snipers, May was determined to utilize her renewed lease on life to the fullest and began volunteering at a soup kitchen. However, she still found time to worry about her nephew Peter, even though she no longer remembered that he was also Spider-Man.

There had been a lot of magic in Spider-Man's life, and to Peter Parker, that wasn't necessarily a good thing. With all his recent encounters with mystical animal spirits and otherworldly demons, Spider-Man was ready to go back to a life more ordinary. But for Peter Parker, that meant the daily life and death struggles of everyone's favorite friendly neighborhood arachnid. Same old power. Same old responsibility. Brand new day.

With his new fresh start, Peter returned to the work he knew best: news photography.

In the wake of his new status quo, Spidey no longer possessed organic webbing, and once again had to use his artificial web-fluid.

AT THE *BUGLE*

With the glamorous life of living in Avengers Tower and working for Tony Stark now behind him, Peter was back to barely making ends meet. He lived in his aunt's house, and attempted to restart his photography career. Meanwhile, *Daily Bugle* publisher J. Jonah Jameson suffered a heart attack, and his wife Marla sold his paper out from under him, worried about the stress it caused him.

Peter Parker made a new life for himself surrounded by friends, including Carlie Cooper and his old buddy Harry Osborn. Although he was fairly broke, he moved out of Aunt May's house and moved in with new acquaintance police officer Vin Gonzales. Vin let Pete move in to win Carlie's favor, unaware that she was secretly interested in Peter.

CARLIE COOPER

Peter met forensic scientist Carlie Cooper through his old friend Harry Osborn. While he instantly liked Carlie, it took Peter a while to realize the extent of his feelings for her.

HARRY OSBORN

While the world believed him dead, Harry Osborn was actually in Europe, as part of an elaborate ruse concocted by his father, Norman. Back in New York, Harry became the owner of the Coffee Bean.

JACKPOT

The new Super Hero Jackpot was a legally registered hero working in Manhattan. Her more than passing resemblance to Mary Jane Watson continually confused Spider-Man.

MEANWHILE...

As Peter struggled to get his life together, Spider-Man was faced with his own set of problems. In the wake of the Super Hero Civil War, many vigilantes were considered outlaws, and could be arrested at any time. Peter had not registered with the government, so he fell into that unfortunate group. While heroes like the newly debuted Jackpot could fight crime without any fear of reprisals, Spidey had to constantly watch his back, knowing that the authorities were looking for an opportunity to take him down.

The situation only worsened when J. Jonah Jameson, having recovered from his heart attack, was elected Mayor of New York City. With the *Daily Bugle* no longer his responsibility, Jameson tried his hand at politics, and used his new power to cause Spider-Man more headaches than ever before. Jameson hired special task forces to take Spidey down, but fortunately Peter stayed one step ahead of the game. Spider-Man constantly made Jameson look foolish by eluding his costly high-tech forces in public, and the newly elected Mayor was eventually forced to call off his relentless war against the web-slinger.

"WE'VE MET. IN ANOTHER LIFE."

MARY JANE

MARY JANE...

Adjusting to the single life was difficult for both Peter and Mary Jane. While Peter spent most of the time alone, Mary Jane had a fling with actor Bobby Carr, before returning to Peter's circle of friends and attempting life on her own.

BRAND NEW THREATS

With his life's new direction and a renewed sense of self, Spider-Man had set out into a Brand New Day. Unfortunately, the so-called Parker Luck came with him, and soon a new breed of Super Villain was appearing all over Manhattan. Spidey's new status quo would come complete with plenty of additions to his rogues gallery.

SCREWBALL

INTERNET SENSATION

The very first live-blogging Super Villain, Screwball set out to gain millions of hits on her website by staging a crime wave and using a webcam to capture the results. With a live feed showcasing her every move, her first encounter with Spider-Man gained her so many extra viewers, she never shied away from crossing his path in the future. A glory hound with the desire to be the next extreme reality star, Screwball is an excellent thief and a master of gymnastics and aerial maneuvers, keeping Spider-Man on his toes and in her camera's sights.

THE ROSE

CRIMINAL LEGACY

When Sara Ehret accidentally injected herself with a virus used in her study of gene therapy, her boss, Dr. Phillip Hayes, was left to deal with the financial fallout from her laboratory accident. While Sara inherited powers and became the Super Hero Jackpot, Dr. Hayes turned to less noble pursuits, and became the newest criminal to adopt the moniker of the Rose in order to regain financial stability. Hayes ordered the criminal Boomerang to murder Sara Ehret's husband, as a message to Jackpot.

MR. NEGATIVE

SPLIT PERSONALITY

By day, Martin Li was an apparent philanthropist and the founder of the soup kitchen where Peter's Aunt May worked. But behind closed doors, he was the new boss of Chinatown's criminal underground. Mr. Negative used his super-power of influence and his army of Inner Demons to create a criminal empire that was eventually exposed by Spider-Man and the second vigilante to take the name Wraith.

MENACE

DEVOTED DAUGHTER

In an attempt to get her father elected as Mayor, Peter's friend and Harry Osborn's fiancée Lily Hollister used the equipment and Goblin Formula that once belonged to Norman Osborn to transform herself into the Super Villain Menace. As Menace, she terrorized her father's campaign, drawing sympathy and support from voters. However, when she was defeated by Spider-Man, her double life ended her father's political career. She later gave birth to Harry's second son before leaving for a life on the run.

FREAK

BEAST OF BURDEN

An addict who would do anything to score his next fix, Freak was born when he stole the donation box from the homeless center where May Parker worked. Tracking down the criminal, Spider-Man webbed him to a rooftop, but the thief got away by shedding his clothes. As he continued to flee, the criminal fell through a glass sunroof, and stumbled upon an experiment in progress by Dr. Curt Connors. Mistaking syringes he discovered for more commonplace illegal drugs, the thief injected himself and became the monstrous being called the Freak.

OVERDRIVE

FAST AND FURIOUS

A thief with the uncanny ability to instantly fuse with and customize any automobile, Overdrive has led Spider-Man on many chases. With just a touch, Overdrive can transform any vehicle to a sleek hotrod capable of near impossible maneuvers. At one point, Overdrive's antics ran him afoul of crime boss Mr. Negative, but the quick-witted thief was able to escape when Mr. Negative's men made the mistake of throwing the villain into the trunk of a car. Overdrive transformed the vehicle into his newest ride, and sped away from the scene.

PAPER DOLL

KILLER CUT-OUT

Paper Doll can flatten her body to razor-thin extremes, possessing the thickness of her namesake. With fingertips so sharp they can even cut Spider-Man's webs to ribbons, Paper Doll stalked the Hollywood actor Bobby Carr, killing those she thought were detrimental to his career. When she targeted Carr's then-girlfriend Mary Jane Watson, Spidey rushed to his ex's rescue, and was able to subdue Doll when she fell in a swimming pool and was forced to regain her three-dimensional shape in a desperate bid for air.

RAPTOR

IN THE WRONG

The former employer of Peter Parker clone Ben Reilly, Dr. Damon Ryder became completely unhinged when he injected himself with dinosaur DNA and killed his wife and children. Ryder adopted the name and costume of the villainous Raptor, and unjustly blamed Ben for the death of his family, even manipulating Ben's old enemy Kaine into helping him achieve his "revenge." Mistaking Peter Parker for his clone, Raptor attacked the innocent Parker several times before Spider-Man was finally able to stop his attacks and bring the criminal to justice.

IRON PATRIOT

Following the events of the Civil War, Spider-Man was now the villain. And Norman Osborn was getting ready to become the hero. With money and power on his side, Osborn geared up to end the menace of his archenemy.

PUTTING THE H.A.M.M.E.R. DOWN

In a shot heard around the world, Norman Osborn, billionaire head of the government agency known as the Thunderbolts, killed the queen of an invading alien force. And just like that, he was America's favorite son. The government handed over the Super Hero forces formerly under Iron Man's control to Osborn, promoting him to head of the peace-keeping organization known as S.H.I.E.L.D. Quickly changing the institution's name to H.A.M.M.E.R., Osborn began to further his own corrupt agenda, which involved hunting down the heroes that he had once come into conflict with when he was the Green Goblin. To that end, Osborn set out to turn himself into a hero. He used Iron Man's technology to create a battlesuit influenced by both Captain America and Iron Man, and become the Iron Patriot. He recruited his own team of faux Avengers, including Venom Mac Gargan, and even convinced the nation that Mac was the true Spider-Man. With his new team in tow, he set out to destroy Captain America's underground rebellion. But all the while, the madness of the Green Goblin was lurking beneath Osborn's calm and collected demeanor.

Finally able to fight back against a lifetime of abuse, Harry Osborn stopped just short of killing his father during their battle.

AMERICAN SON

It wasn't long before Norman Osborn decided that he wanted to recruit his son Harry into the family business. Using Harry's former fiancée, the heavily pregnant Lily Hollister, as a pawn in his game, Osborn was able to convince Harry to take up the mantle of the armored American Son as he believed Lily's child was his.

However when Norman captured and was about to kill Spider-Man, Harry saw his father for the true monster that he was. He geared up in his American Son armor and bested his father in a violent clash. But rather than kill Norman and become as bad as his father, Harry decided to walk away and Norman was left without a son. However, he had won the heart of Lily Hollister, and planned to raise her son as the new heir to his twisted throne.

When Norman used government forces to storm Asgard, claiming it was a security threat, the world saw the extent of his madness and corruption. He was jailed and the Superhuman Registration Act was lifted, but only after Spidey got a little payback.

THE GAUNTLET

The villains were crawling out of the woodwork. Several of Spider-Man's old foes like Electro and the Lizard were getting power upgrades while dangerous faces like the new Vulture and Rhino were trying to replace other familiar rogues. Spider-Man was running a gauntlet of sorts, and was quickly reaching the point of exhaustion.

THE GRIM HUNT

Kraven the Hunter had died years ago by his own hand. But his family wasn't quite so ready to give up on the violent Kravinoff legacy. So they watched Spider-Man from the shadows, and slowly planned his death.

> "THEY'RE HUNTING US... THEY'RE HUNTING SPIDERS."
> KAINE

Kaine weakly made his way to Peter Parker's apartment, covered in his own blood and barely alive. He had to warn Peter of the coming danger.

WAR ON SPIDERS

Spider-Man felt as weak as a kitten. Running a gauntlet of his old foes and battling one almost immediately after the next had caught up with him. He was sick in bed with swine flu when he was surprised by his clone Kaine, close to death, but there to warn him that someone was hunting "spiders."

Spider-Man was then called into action when he heard an explosion nearby, and chanced upon Arachne being hunted by Kraven's children Ana and Alyosha. Spider-Man succeeded in saving Arachne's life, and the two fled to the nearest safe house Arachne could think of, the ransacked apartment of former Spider-Woman Mattie Franklin. There they encountered Spider-Man's old spider-powered mentor Ezekiel, apparently back from the dead. Ezekiel told the heroes of a prophesized war between Hunters and Spiders. The Kravens' next target would be Araña. Arachne and Spider-Man tracked down Araña, but they were overpowered by the Kravens, and Arachne and Araña were kidnapped. Ezekiel and Spider-Man traveled north of the city to pursue the Kravens, but it was a trap. Ezekiel was actually the Chameleon, Kraven's half-brother, in disguise.

Spider-Man thought the deceased Ezekiel was magically drawn to the fray due to being a fellow "spider," but he was the Chameleon in disguise.

The Kravens had kidnapped Mattie Franklin and Madame Web. Kraven's wife Sasha stabbed Mattie in the chest, and used her blood in an arcane ritual to resurrect Kraven's son, Vladimir, the Grim Hunter.

Led into a trap by the Chameleon, Spider-Man was ambushed by the Kraven family, falling into an open grave before being stabbed on Kraven's altar.

KRAVEN REBORN

A second chance at life was the last thing that Kraven wanted, having felt he had achieved the ultimate victory in defeating Spider-Man before taking his own life. However, he had no choice in the matter. When Spider-Man was lured to the Kraven estate, stabbed, and apparently killed, his blood triggered an alchemical spell, and the original Kraven the Hunter was returned to the living. Unlike Kraven's son Vladimir, who had returned to life as a hideous man-lion mutation due to the use of Mattie Franklin's "impure" blood, Kraven was in perfect health, seemingly from the pure essence of the spider that Peter Parker's body contained. But despite his physical condition, Kraven knew that the ritual was an abomination of nature, and something about it wasn't right.

Examining Spider-Man's body, Kraven realized that it wasn't the true spider that had brought him back. It was Spider-Man's clone, Kaine. When Peter Parker had fallen into the empty grave during his battle with Kraven's family, Kaine had buried Spider-Man to ensure that he would stay out of harm's way, and had taken his place in the grave.

Later, Peter regained his senses and climbed his way out of the earth. After discovering Kaine's body beside his old black costume and a note that read "Hunt me," Spider-Man complied with Kraven's wishes, angrily taking his fight directly to Kraven's family. He took the Kravens down one at a time, but was too late to save Madame Web from Sasha Kraven's wrath. Sasha killed the fortune teller, and Web passed her prophetic gift on to Arachne. And after the dust settled, and the casualties were counted, a familiar face emerged from the ground. It seemed that even death couldn't stop the force of nature that was Kaine.

Kraven was disgusted by his resurrection, and believed his wife Sasha had made a mockery of his accomplishments.

Besting Kraven, Spider-Man stood over the villain, preparing to kill his old foe. But after Arachne showed the web-slinger a glimpse of the horrible future that would evolve out of Kraven's death, Spidey stayed his hand.

February 2011

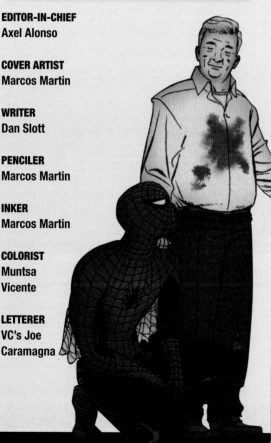

THE AMAZING SPIDER-MAN #655

"I swear to you... from now on... whenever I'm around, wherever I am, no-one dies!"

SPIDER-MAN

EDITOR-IN-CHIEF
Axel Alonso

COVER ARTIST
Marcos Martin

WRITER
Dan Slott

PENCILER
Marcos Martin

INKER
Marcos Martin

COLORIST
Muntsa Vicente

LETTERER
VC's Joe Caramagna

MAIN CHARACTERS: Spider-Man; J. Jonah Jameson; Marla Jameson

MAIN SUPPORTING CHARACTERS: Joe Robertson; Martha Robertson; Ben Urich; Randy Robertson; Carlie Cooper; Max Modell; Jay Jameson; Aunt May Jameson; Glory Grant; Betty Brant; various deceased people from Spider-Man's past; Captain Yuri Watanabe

MAIN LOCATIONS: J. Jonah Jameson's home; Peter Parker's apartment; the *Daily Bugle* office; St. Patrick's Cathedral, New York City; unnamed cemetery; a New York City bank

BACKGROUND

The Brand New Day in Spider-Man's life had come and gone, but its themes and concepts had formed the foundation of Spider-Man's revised and slightly reinvented universe. Among the changes was an emphasis on story over event. This new approach was in good hands with talented big-name writers such as Joe Kelly and Mark Waid. Meanwhile, the Spider-Man editorial offices were taking chances with the artistic approach by hiring artists who were previously rarely used on mainstream projects due to their original styles, to give each story a unique and imaginative feel.

Chief among those artists was Marcos Martin. With a simplistic yet intricate style, Martin seemed tailor-made for Spider-Man. And nowhere was that more apparent than in *The Amazing Spider-Man* #655, in which Martin got the chance to shine with a sequence of somber silent panels and a surreal dream world. Combined with Dan Slott's script, the issue was powerful, moving, and a perfect example of placing story above all else.

THE STORY

After attending the funeral of J. Jonah Jameson's wife, Peter Parker experiences a harrowing dream populated by all those who Spider-Man had been unable to save.

J. Jonah Jameson's alarm went off at 7:00 a.m., but he didn't need it. The former publisher of the *Daily Bugle* was finding it hard to get any sleep (**1**). He just lay there in his now all-too-empty bed, next to where his wife used to rest. But Marla Jameson was gone now, and Jonah had to get on with his day. So he got up, showered and shaved—and headed to his wife's funeral.

Peter Parker wasn't doing much better, and neither was the staff at the *Bugle* for that matter. But nevertheless they all made their way to St. Patrick's Cathedral in Manhattan, and sat through the terribly sad proceedings (**2**). Later at the cemetery, Jameson looked on as his wife's coffin was lowered into the ground (**3**). Peter watched his former boss walk away from his wife's fresh plot. But Peter's mind wasn't just on Marla Jameson and Jonah's loss. And when he went to sleep in his lonely apartment that night, Peter's true thoughts began to emerge (**4**).

He didn't stop the Burglar. Peter was living it all again as if it were yesterday. In a haunting dream, Peter was confronted by his Uncle Ben and then by his faceless, dead parents (**5**). To make matters worse, Ben's murderer was sitting down with all of them at the kitchen table in Peter's childhood home (**6**). And then suddenly, Marla Jameson greeted him.

Peter followed Marla through the dream and into a bizarre cityscape populated by the dead faces from his past (**7**). There were dozens of them, all people Spider-Man just couldn't save. From Aunt May's former love Nathan Lubensky, to the Scarlet Spider, to Gwen Stacy. From police detective Jean DeWolff to *Bugle* reporter Fredrick Foswell to businessman Ezekiel. It was a haunting laundry list of ghosts and phantoms from times past. And it brought Peter Parker to his knees.

All of a sudden he was back on a twisted version of the George Washington Bridge, staring down the Green Goblin with the lifeless Gwen hanging limply in the monster's arms (**8**). And then he was being pulled down into the hard split earth by Kraven's dead hand (**9**). Suddenly he was in a pub watching Scourge and the Punisher callously murder a few forgettable Super Villains. Then before he knew it, he was watching helplessly as the Sentry ripped Carnage in half while flying through outer space. And then he was backstage at that TV studio again as the Burglar ran past him.

But this time, Spider-Man wasn't going to let him get away. This time, the hero raised his fist and beat the soon-to-be killer into a pulp. But it wasn't the Burglar he'd beaten—it was his Uncle Ben.

Looking down at the bloody body of the man who raised him, Spider-Man swore that it would never come to this. That he wouldn't be responsible for the death of everything Ben had taught him. And from behind him, a woman's voice sounded. Marla Jameson was asking Spider-Man what he would do now (**10**).

Peter woke up in a cold sweat (**11**). He put on his Spider-Man costume and headed to greet the dawn from a nearby rooftop (**12**). He knew what he had to do. He made his city a promise that whenever he was around, no one else would die.

At a bank across town, a villain called Massacre had different ideas. Holding innocent people hostage, he proved that he had no regard for human life. With the simple squeeze of a trigger, he made a mockery of Spider-Man's new oath in an instant.

"If that's so, then tell us... what will you do now?"

MARLA JAMESON

AFTERWORD

Stan Lee chose the perfect adjective for his hero, that much is for sure. When you look at the popularity Spider-Man has maintained since his debut, there's simply no better way to describe his career—it's nothing short of amazing.

Take a minute and ask yourself: who are the top three Super Heroes in comics? The answer is obvious: Superman, Batman, and Spider-Man. All three are indisputably iconic, incredibly popular, and each has become a franchise in its own right. That in itself is a near-impossible achievement in the world's crowded marketplace, but when you look to the characters' histories, you'll find something even more impressive.

Superman debuted in 1938. Batman was released the following year. Spider-Man didn't make his first appearance in comics until 1962. That's nearly two and a half decades later. Two and a half decades that were jam-packed with nearly every Super Hero concept imaginable. There were even several spider-themed heroes, including the DC Comics character Tarantula and the Quality Comics character Alias the Spider.

So why did Spider-Man shine while those arachnid-inspired heroes fell into the realm of comic book obscurity? The answer is pretty simple. It wasn't about the spider at all. It was about the man. Stan Lee dared enough to add a new dimension to his web-slinging Super Hero. He gave us Peter Parker, a man who led an unlucky life, complete with various problems and missteps. And the perfect world of comics began to look a little bit more like our own—albeit laced with elements of the fantastic. The real appeal of reading *The Amazing Spider-Man* was getting to know Peter Parker, and the response to the character was overwhelming.

It might not be the most original statement when I say that Spider-Man is easily my favorite Marvel hero. Nevertheless, that fact did make this book pretty fun to write. While I'm on the subject, I'd like to thank both my editors Laura Gilbert and Helen Murray for their enthusiastic work on this project, as well as the many designers on DK's team. I'd also like to thank my wife Dorothy and daughter Lillian, for their tolerance of the many hours I spent locked away in my office reading and writing. And this book would be just half as long without the original text by the great Tom DeFalco, who literally wrote not only the book on Spidey, but also many of the comics that the book was based on.

Last but not least, thanks to Stan Lee, for creating not just Spider-Man, but also Peter Parker. Because truth be told, Spider-Man isn't the most important part. Lee could have designed his hero based on pretty much any other animal or heroic theme. He could have been named Walrus-Man, yet as long as the face behind the mask belonged to Peter Parker, the result would have been the same. It would still be amazing.

Matthew K. Manning
Mystic, Connecticut

Senior Editors Laura Gilbert, Helen Murray
Editors Jo Casey, Matt Jones
Senior Jacket and Slipcase Designer Mark Penfound
Senior Designer David McDonald
Senior Art Editors Guy Harvey, Rajnish Kashyap
Art Editors Nico Alba, Akanksha Gupta, Lisa Sodeau
Designers Owen Bennett, Lauren Rosier
Design Assistant Rhys Thomas
Producer Naomi Green
Pre-Production Producer Kavita Varma
Senior Designer and Brand Manager Robert Perry
Managing Editor Sadie Smith
Design Manager Ron Stobbart
Creative Manager Sarah Harland
Art Director Lisa Lanzarini
Publisher Julie Ferris
Publishing Director Simon Beecroft

This edition published in 2016
First published in Great Britain in 2015
by Dorling Kindersley Limited
80 Strand, London, WC2R 0RL

This edition produced for the Book People Ltd,
Hall Wood Avenue, Haydock, St Helen's, WA11 9UL

Contains content first published in
*Spider–Man: Inside the World of Your Friendly
Neighbourhood Hero* (2012)

Slipcase UI: 001-297741-May/2016

marvel.com

A CIP catalogue record for this book
is available from the British Library.

ISBN: 978-0-2412-4276-6

Printed in China.

The publisher would like to thank Shari Last for editorial
assistance; Neil Kelly for editorial assistance; Anjan Dey and
Era Chawla for design assistance; Chelsea Alon, Rich Thomas,
Scott Piehl, and Lauren Kressel from Disney Publishing;
Ruwan Jayatilleke and Kelly Lamy from Marvel.

www.dk.com

A WORLD OF IDEAS:
SEE ALL THERE IS TO KNOW